Must
We Fight?

Must
We Fight?

*From the Battlefield
to the Schoolyard—
A New Perspective
on Violent Conflict
and Its Prevention*

William L. Ury, Editor

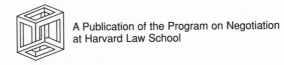

A Publication of the Program on Negotiation
at Harvard Law School

JOSSEY-BASS
A Wiley Company
www.josseybass.com

Published by

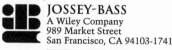

JOSSEY-BASS
A Wiley Company
989 Market Street
San Francisco, CA 94103-1741

| www.josseybass.com |

Jossey-Bass books and products are available through most bookstores. To contact Jossey-Bass directly, call (888) 378-2537, fax to (800) 605-2665, or visit our website at www.josseybass.com.

Substantial discounts on bulk quantities of Jossey-Bass books are available to corporations, professional associations, and other organizations. For details and discount information, contact the special sales department at Jossey-Bass.

We at Jossey-Bass strive to use the most environmentally sensitive paper stocks available to us. Our publications are printed on acid-free recycled stock whenever possible, and our paper always meets or exceeds minimum GPO and EPA requirements.

Library of Congress Cataloging-in-Publication Data
Must we fight? : from the battlefield to the schoolyard, a new perspective on violent conflict and its prevention / William L. Ury, editor. — 1st ed.
    p. cm.
"A publication of the Program on Negotiation at Harvard Law School."
Includes bibliographical references.
Contents: Primate behavior and human aggression / Frans de Waal — The history of war : fact vs. fiction / R. Brian Ferguson — The power of the "third side" : community roles in conflict resolution / William L. Ury — Reducing youth violence in Boston : lessons from the 1990s / Christopher Winship — Reducing Hindu-Muslim violence in Indian towns : community initiatives / Steven Wilkinson — Containing, resolving, and preventing violent conflict : activating the third side in urban communities / William L. Ury — Questions, comments, answers — Sanford High race riot : opportunities and choices for the third side / Joshua Weiss, Brian Blancke, and Chang In Shin.

ISBN 0-7879-6103-5 (alk. paper)

1. Conflict management. 2. Social conflict—Prevention. 3. Violence—Prevention. I. Ury, William. II. Program on Negotiation at Harvard Law School.

HM1126 .M87 2001
303.6'9--dc21   2001006812

first edition
HB Printing 10 9 8 7 6 5 4 3 2 1

Contents

About the Authors

William L. Ury, editor, is co-author of the best-selling *Getting to YES* and author of *Getting Past No.* His latest book is *The Third Side: Why We Fight and How We Can Stop* (2000) previously published as *Getting to Peace: Transforming Conflict at Home, at Work, and in the World* (1999). Dr. Ury is director of the Project on Preventing War at PON and a member of its Steering Committee. A newly created Web site, thirdside.org., is designed to stimulate discussion of the ideas in these books.

Brian Blancke, a PhD candidate at Syracuse University and an affiliate of the Program on the Analyses and Resolution of Conflicts (PARC), is conducting research in settling Cayuga Indian Nation land claims through negotiation. Brian was a PON Graduate Research Fellow for 2000-2001.

Frans de Waal of Emory University has extensively studied conflict resolution in nonhuman primates. He received the *Los Angeles Times* Book Award for *Peacemaking among Primates* (1989), a popularized account of 15 years of research on this topic.

R. Brian Ferguson of Rutgers University-Newark is one of the leading anthropologists of war. He is the editor, with Neil Whitehead, of *War in the Tribal Zone: Expanding States and Indigenous Warfare* (1992) and author of *Yanomami Warfare: A Political History* (1995).

Chang In Shin, a PhD candidate at Pennsylvania State University, is studying the international trade negotiations between Korea and China as a context for examining the role of culture and identity in negotiation. Chang was a PON Graduate Research Fellow for 2000-2001.

Joshua Weiss, a PhD candidate at George Mason University, is pursuing a critique of "gradualism" as the dominant strategy behind negotiation toward the implementation of peace processes attempting to end communal conflict. Josh was a PON Graduate Research Fellow for 2000-2001.

Steven Wilkinson, assistant professor of Political Science at Duke University, specializes in the study of ethnic conflict, especially the relationship between electoral competition and ethnic violence in countries such as India, Malaysia and Ireland. He has written on the role of the media in ethnic conflict and on the lack of effectiveness of "consociational" power-sharing agreements. His recent work explains why apparently similar towns and states in India have very different levels of Hindu-Muslim violence.

Christopher Winship is chair of the Department of Sociology at Harvard University. For the past six years he has been working with and studying the Ten-Point Coalition. His latest publication in this area is *Boston Cops and Black Churches* (The Public Interest, 1999), written with Jenny Berrien. His research interests include religion and public policy, statistical models for qualitative data, the estimation of causal effects with nonexperimental data, the effects of education on mental ability, and changes in the racial composition of prisons.

Preface

The Third Side Symposia at Harvard

No human problem is more pressing or more challenging than that of violence, the bodily harm that individuals, groups, and nations inflict on one another in the course of their conflicts. Tragically, violence abounds from school shootings to genocidal wars, from Columbine to Kosovo.

The questions naturally arise: Is violence an inherent and inevitable part of human life? Can it be prevented? In short, *must we fight?*

In October 1999 and September 2000, the Program on Negotiation at Harvard Law School held two public symposia in which scholars from different disciplines sought to address these questions.

The first symposium, entitled "Violent human nature? Telling a new story," focused on new scientific insights into the human capacity for violence and peacemaking. "Human nature" is often invoked in political deliberation and popular discourse to explain brutal violence and why so little can be done to prevent it. Recent investigations in the fields of primatology, anthropology, and conflict resolution suggest quite a different picture of human nature with powerful implications for how we can prevent violence and wars today.

The meeting brought together representatives of three disciplines, each with a different lens on violence and human nature. Professor Frans de Waal of Emory University, an eminent primatologist, presented his research on aggression and reconciliation among primates. Professor Brian Ferguson of Rutgers University, a leading authority on the anthropology of war, described the archaeological evidence for early violence and war. Lastly, from the vantage point of conflict resolution, I offered some speculations about how our early ancestors may have dealt with their conflicts using the intervention of the surrounding community, the "Third Side."

7

The second symposium was entitled "The Third Side: Mobilizing Communities to Prevent Urban Violence." Professor Christopher Winship of Harvard University began by describing how a group of African-American ministers worked successfully together with the police to prevent youth violence in Boston. Professor Steven Wilkinson of Duke University presented the case of several Indian cities that effectively prevented ethnic riots between Hindus and Muslims that killed hundreds in other cities. Drawing on these two very different case studies for illustration, I presented a conceptual framework revolving around the "Third Side."

Together, we examined three major questions in this second symposium:

1. What factors enabled the community in these cases to help prevent violence? What were the obstacles and how were they overcome?
2. How did the community—the Third Side—become mobilized? What were the motivations for people to get involved despite considerable costs and risks?
3. What generalizable lessons can we draw for preventing violent conflict in other communities around the world?

Responsive audiences raised a number of other questions of their own, helping to further explore and expand the concept of the Third Side at all levels of human interaction.

If the first symposium focused on the past and served to bring out a new and different story of human conflict, the second symposium dwelt on the present and looked at the practical modalities by which violent conflict can be prevented. Together, both symposia raised important questions bearing on the future of human violence.

The first two parts of this publication are edited transcriptions of the two symposia presentations and the question-and-answer period that followed the 2000 meeting. The style is naturally that of the spoken, not the written, word.

The last part of this book is a "Third Side" simulation designed for classroom use. Based on actual events, the simulation asks students to put themselves in the place of an administrator faced with a community conflict, in this case, a racial incident at a public high school. The three authors were graduate research fellows at the Program on Negotiation during 2000-2001: Brian Blancke, Chang In Shin, and Joshua Weiss.

The two symposia, the thoughtful questions of the audience, and the simulation are collected here to stimulate thinking among students, theorists, and practitioners about the Third Side and how it might be used to prevent, contain, and resolve conflict.

Let me end by expressing my deep gratitude to all those who made this book a reality. First thanks go to my colleagues Frans de Waal, Brian Ferguson, Christopher Winship, and Steve Wilkinson, who took time out of their busy schedules to participate actively in the symposia and to present their fascinating research. The symposia were ably and graciously convened by Sara Cobb, then executive director of the Program on Negotiation. The Program offered generous financial and organizational support for the project. Terry Hill, director of PON Publications, skillfully edited the transcripts and handled the publication process from beginning to end. Final thanks go to my family, Lizanne, Chris, Tommy, and Gabi, thirdsiders all, for their patience, love, and support.

William L. Ury
Cambridge, Massachusetts
October 2001

PART I

Violent Human Nature: Telling a New Story

William L. Ury

In this past year when it came to the question of intervening in Kosovo, as in Bosnia or Rwanda, we heard countless times in the media that these people have been fighting for centuries and centuries; it's in their blood and there's nothing you can do about it. The day after the Columbine shooting in April 1999, the spokesperson for the school district was quoted as saying, "You can take every reasonable step to make a positive environment for everyone, but sometimes human nature will defeat you." This attribution of violence and war to human nature has a rich intellectual heritage. Voltaire, for instance, expressed the widespread beliefs of his time when he asserted that slavery is as ancient as war and was human nature. At the beginning of this century, Freud posited the existence of an instinct of destruction and aggression, believing that it lay at the root of war. He wrote, "Under primitive conditions it is superior force, brute violence or violence backed by arms, that lords it everywhere."

Just after the Second World War, the anthropologist Raymond Dart wrote a series of influential papers elaborating a theory that human beings had evolved as killers and cannibals. In his language, "The blood bespattered slaughter-gutted archives of human history, from the earliest Egyptian or Sumerian records to the most recent atrocities of the Second World War, accord with early universal cannibalism in proclaiming this common bloodlust differentiator, this predacious habit, this mark of Cain." It turned out that the archaeological evidence on which Raymond Dart based his theory was mistaken, the persuasive rebuttal coming from a scientist with a fitting name of Brain, Bob Brain. But it didn't matter.

11

The American writer Robert Ardrey had already publicized Dart's conception of humans as killer apes around the world in a series of best-selling books. And more recently, the notion that war has genetic roots has been extensively written about by sociobiologists among others.

Nor is this issue of violence and human nature debated just in academia. The academic evidence is often cited in the public policy debate. For example, a recent article in *Foreign Affairs* by Francis Fukuyama began with accounts of chimpanzees killing other chimpanzees and accounts of prehistoric violence. So it matters.

The purpose of our symposium is to examine these commonly-expressed beliefs about the connection between violence and human nature; to discuss what we know and what we don't know; to present a different story, perhaps, than the conventional one of our primate and prehistoric heritage; and to draw some practical implications of this different story for dealing with today's conflicts.

The story of violent human nature is based on three things usually: on our knowledge of chimps and other primates; on the archaeological record; and on our knowledge of simple societies—the ones whose way of life most closely resembles that of our ancestors. In the first discussion, Professor de Waal explains what we know about primate behavior. Professor Ferguson provides insights from the archaeological record and the anthropology of war. My remarks about conflict resolution focus on some of the simplest societies on earth, as well as on the implications of these presentations for dealing with violence and wars today.

On a personal note, I just want to acknowledge my intellectual debt to both Professor de Waal and Professor Ferguson. It's an honor to be sharing a forum with them. This is perhaps the first time that these three fields—primatology, anthropology, and conflict resolution—have come together to outline what might be a more accurate story of where we come from and some implications for where we're going.

12

Primate Behavior and Human Aggression

Frans de Waal

In my field, the discussion of aggression started to a large degree with Konrad Lorenz, an Austrian ethologist who worked mainly on fish and geese and who had a very Freudian perspective on aggression. He saw aggression as a drive. He wrote his book *On Aggression* and defined it in a way that was very important, because at that time there was confusion between predation and aggression. Humans as carnivores were equated with humans as aggressors. Of course, many carnivores such as wolves have a very highly evolved social system and are not necessarily more aggressive than some noncarnivores. Lorenz explained that when a cat stalks a mouse, it's not necessarily in an aggressive mood but may be motivated by something else, such as hunger. So Lorenz took these two things apart and defined aggression as the fighting instinct in beast and man which is directed against members of the same species.

This clarified a lot about aggressive behavior. And at the same time it created an enormous controversy, because the innate drive model of aggression opened a whole research agenda for a lot of people, particularly psychologists working in the US, who wanted to show that aggression is learned. However, demonstrating that aggression is learned, as they did, does not demonstrate that it's nongenetic. That was the mistake of that time, of the 1960s and '70s; I hope we're not going to make that mistake here because one doesn't exclude the other.

We now don't believe that aggression is necessarily the same as, let's say, hunger. Hunger builds up and you have to eat at some point. That's not necessarily how we look at aggression. Aggression is triggered by particular situations. If these situations don't occur, aggression doesn't need to occur.

The killer ape myth is older than Lorenz and started, as was just mentioned in Bill Ury's introduction, with Raymond Dart who, on very flimsy fossil evidence, built his case that we were killer apes. The idea was then popularized by Robert Ardrey. Calhoun, who worked with rats, found that crowded rats fight a lot. Ardrey interpreted this to mean that people crowded into inner cities will behave very similarly to crowded rats. I've done a lot of research demonstrating that crowding and aggression are not necessarily closely related in the human species, or in primate species. Desmond Morris in *The Naked Ape* (1969) also built on this story, which became sort of consistent: We are born aggressors. We are instinctively aggressive.

Initially there was quite a bit of resistance, because the ape story didn't fit. The apes were seen as peaceful vegetarians who moved from tree to tree and didn't do anything but eat and sleep and groom each other. But when Jane Goodall in the late 1970s found her chimpanzees fighting and even killing each other, it strengthened the aggressive primate story.

I call this the internal generation model—still the dominant one—of aggression, meaning that it looks at aggressive behavior as something that is generated internally in the individual, either by a drive, by hormones, by genes, by learning, by models on TV, or by frustration. Aggression is generated internally and then has to come out, with terrible results. I will explain why I don't necessarily think that way.

Let me say, I don't think that all these ideas are wrong. I'm not saying that these connections don't exist. But most of the aggression that we see occurs in a social context. As an example of studies that ignored this context, the early studies on aggression on rats involved shock-induced aggression—basically frustration pain-induced aggression. Researchers would take two rats who didn't know each other, put them on a grid, and then shock them. The rats would, so to speak, blame each other for the shock. Their attacks on each other were induced by the pain

14

that they got. This has nothing to do with real-life rat behavior; it has very little to do with social relationships; and it's in the social relationships that most aggression occurs.

I will be talking mainly about individuals who know each other and who live *within* a group. I'm not saying that the story that I'm telling applies to what happens *between* groups. I think that out-group aggression is different from in-group aggression. I will talk mainly about what happens within the group; but still it serves as a reminder that not everything that occurs is purely competitive in animal groups, and that aggression can be understood as part of social relationships.

When I started working on aggressive behavior in macaques, I found that if you look, over time, at a macaque group, you find little clusters of aggression. Less than five percent of the macacque time budget is devoted to aggressive behavior—in between there are enormous periods of play and grooming during which the macaques get along fine. So I got interested in the alternation between the two states: How is it possible that animals who occasionally have fierce battles among themselves nevertheless seem to get along? How does this work? I didn't really resolve that with the macaques, but when I started working with chimpanzees I started seeing a pattern.

Aggression is not unusual for the chimpanzee, especially in captivity, but also in the field. What happens afterwards is interesting, and I started calling this a "reconciliation," defined as a friendly contact between two former opponents not long after a conflict. The "not long" part is really just for practical reasons. It's very hard to work on these animals and to look for reconciliations that occur a week later. We know that with people, reconciliations can occur a generation following a conflict. Another type of behavior, "consolation," is defined as friendly contact provided by a bystander to the aggressed party. I won't get much into the consolation part, but it's very interesting as well.

Chimpanzees not only reconcile with each other; they also mediate in reconciliations. For example, take the situation of two males who have been in a fight. Although they live on a very large island where it's very easy to avoid each other, they sit opposite each other and avoid eye contact. If one looks up, the other one will look at the sky, and vice versa. It's a sort of situation that Bill Ury probably deals with quite a bit. They need a negotiator.

What happens sometimes in chimpanzees is that a female will approach one of the two. Usually an older female, she will groom the male for a while, and after she has done that she will get up and walk very slowly to the other male, and the first male will walk right behind her so he doesn't need to make eye contact with the opponent. And if he doesn't walk, we have seen females turn around and grab his arm and make him walk. This indicates an intentional process on the part of the female. Then she may groom the other male; the three of them sit together; and then after a while she leaves and the two males continue grooming. She has brought the two parties together.

There are two interesting aspects to this. One is the cognitive aspect: The female needs to understand something of the social process that has happened between these males and why they are stuck, so to speak, in a certain pattern, and how she can fix it. A whole lot of cognition goes into this. The other part is the motivation aspect. Why is she doing this? She's taking a risk, because this is a very tense situation. Maybe that's why it's mainly done by older females who know this sort of stuff much better than the younger ones. What motivates her to take this risk? I think this sort of problem fixing within a community is related to the evolution of morality. It expresses a certain concern about the state of affairs within the community, which I have termed "community concern."

The word "reconciliation" is, of course, borrowed from human language. Some people would say it's an anthropomorphism that you shouldn't be using for animals. I personally have no problems using anthropomorphisms because I believe that if two closely related species show very similar behavior under very similar circumstances, the burden of proof will be on others to show me that it's differently motivated or differently processed. I assume that if chimpanzees, who are so close to us, do something that looks almost identical to what we do under similar circumstances, we can assume as a default position that the motivations underlying it are very similar as well. Reconciliation is basically a heuristic concept, a label which by itself can never be sufficient. If you use a term as loaded as "reconciliation," you will want to support it in some way.

Reconciliation studies in primates have been going on for the last 20 years, and there are currently maybe 50 people active. There are papers coming out on a regular basis. A lot of people have been testing the whole range of predictions that we derived from the reconciliation concept, predictions such as, if reconciliation really is what we think it is, it should repair relationships. It should reduce future aggression; it should restore tolerance; it should reduce anxiety; it should occur especially between individuals who do have relationships that they value. And almost all the predictions that I know of have been supported one way or another by data now coming out of the field and also data from experimental settings; most of it comes from observation in captive settings.

This is the way it's usually tested. It's called the PC/MC method, for "post-conflict and a matched-control" observation. Let's say there's a 10-minute observation window after a fight, and you measure how often individuals get together after a fight, for example, say 50 percent of the pairs of opponents make friendly contact after the fight. Then you do a control observation on the same individuals at the same time of day but on a different occasion. What we find is an increased tendency for contact after conflict between individuals. Exactly counter to the sort of theory I grew up with in the 1970s.

17

In the 1970s, aggression was depicted as a dispersive mechanism, which drives individuals apart and increases the distance between them. This type of theory coming out of Lorenzian and other thinking applied very well to territorial species such as many fish and birds. But social animals, of course, couldn't live that way. If your life depends on a social group and every conflict increases distance, what are you going to end up with? You're going to end up living alone. That's not a possibility for animals who live in social groups and who depend on each other for cooperation. They need a totally different process and that's what we see here. We actually see *attraction* between opponents after fights.

This has become the dominant hypothesis of the field, and I think it's reasonably to very well-supported. It basically says that reconciliation will occur especially between individuals who stand much to lose if their relationship deteriorates. This is a hypothesis very familar to Europeans, because the European Community is based on it. The European Community was formed after the war to prevent future warfare between countries who had been fighting for quite a while. The idea was that if we foster economic ties between these countries, thus making their relationships valuable, we may be able to reduce conflict between them. The studies on primates indicate this same sort of connection. There are some experimental studies, very elegant ones actually, by Marina Cords that support this connection; and also observational studies.

I think that the reconciliation mechanism has been found in 25 different primates now, and people have started looking beyond the primates, because if the valuable-relationship hypothesis is correct, there's no reason to expect that it's limited to chimpanzees or monkeys or whatever. There are many animal species, dolphins, elephants, wolves, you name it, who have cooperative relationships but do have conflicts among themselves at the same time. They need some sort of mechanism to maintain the cooperation despite the conflicting interests that exist.

There's evidence now that domestic goats and dolphins and hyenas and I suppose a number of other species have processes similar to reconciliation in primates. I wouldn't be surprised if it's actually quite widespread and will be found in many, many different species.

The bonobo is an interesting primate. I'm bringing them up here because we have the impression that we are killer apes, that chimpanzees are killer apes, and that we have been killing each other for five million years. We probably have—I don't want to deny that—but maybe not at the scale that we're thinking about. The bonobo, which is just as close to us as the chimpanzee, is important to bring into this picture.

The bonobo is a very appealing primate. It was discovered in 1929 as a separate species and has been studied in the field only since the mid-'70s. It has not been studied extensively in captivity, because there are only 110 of them captive in the whole world, as opposed to thousands of chimpanzees. We know much less about the bonobo than about the chimpanzee, but what we know indicates that had the bonobo been discovered and studied first, we would have very different theories about ourselves. These are the great apes—the gorilla and a number of subspecies; the orangutan and a number of subspecies; and then Pan, one genus with two species: the bonobo and the chimpanzee with three subspecies. The bonobo is a very close relative of the chimpanzee.

Chimpanzees are extremely strong compared to people; they have very powerful shoulders on a thick neck and a big head. A lot of weight is shifted to the upper body compared to the bonobo. The bonobo has much narrower shoulders; a black face with a gorilla-like nose and reddish lips; and a lot of weight has shifted to the back of the body, to the legs. They have longer legs, and when they walk bipedally they look more like an *Australopithecus,* to which they have been compared. They look very human-like. They also straighten their back better, it seems, than the chimpanzee. Of course, they're not human-like at all in their feet. The feet are the feet of an arboreal primate.

The bonobo, although clearly related to the chimpanzee, is anatomically quite different and behaviorally even more so. If we had not known anything about chimpanzees and bonobos and had found only the skulls and the bones of these animals, as usually happens in the fossil record, no one would have suspected the enormous differences in behavior that we see. So I just send this out as a little warning to those who, on the basis of three bones that they find somewhere, make enormous conclusions about behavior.

Everything that the chimpanzee does with kissing and embracing, the bonobo does with sexual activities. So they best fit the sort of image of apes that existed in the 17th century. Bonobos not only have frontal copulations; they have a lot of exchange of emotions. Sex doesn't occur only between males and females; sex occurs in all combinations of individuals. For example, females engage in what is called gg rubbing, or genito-genital rubbing. They rub their genital swellings together and have sexual contact.

The bonobo is a species where sex is used to resolve conflict; it's really a make-love-not-war kind of species in which sex occurs in all combinations of individuals. And that has to do with the fact that tensions occur in all combinations of individuals. It's a bonding mechanism; and for females it's actually very important because it's also a political mechanism. The females dominate the males in bonobo society, and they do this to a large degree by bonding. They do it by means of alliances that rest on the sort of bonding mechanisms that occur between the females. You can see why the bonobo has become a favorite of feminists and homosexuals.

I think it's a species that handles conflict in principle in the same way as chimpanzees, because chimpanzees have also their reconciliations and their bonding mechanisms and so on. But bonobos seem to do so more effectively. At least in captivity, if you look at how many reconciliations occur, chimpanzees reconcile about 30 percent of their conflicts, and bonobos about 50 percent of their conflicts. The reconciliation rate is higher; and the violence rate seems to be lower. For example, infanticide has been reported for chimpanzees in the field, but has not been seen in bonobos. Intergroup aggression, aggression between different communities, has been seen in chimpanzees. In bonobos, the opposite has been seen—we have seen intergroup mingling which involves a lot of sexual contact between the females of different groups, and also sexual contact with males in other groups. That sort of thing has never been seen in chimpanzees. That's a sort of absolute difference. I'm not saying that there's no real or possible hostility between bonobo groups, but lethal aggression has not been seen, and intergroup mingling has, which is not known among chimpanzees.

There seem to be some fundamental differences, in the sense that the bonobo is a more peaceful species, reconciles more easily, and does so in a sexual manner. That makes them sort of interesting for the killer-ape story, because one can argue that we have two relatives equally close to us: One of them has more violent propensities than the other one. I'm not saying that it is necessary to choose between the two. The need for a model for ourselves is the sort of quest in anthropology that I've never understood. Anthropologists have been looking for human models, e.g., "This is the sort of primitive society that we should look at." The same has happened in the primate literature, e.g., "Is the chimpanzee or the bonobo the better model?" A lot of wishful thinking can go into the bonobo model, for example. But I don't think we need to choose; we need to take all the information we can get, from the chimp, the bonobo, the gorilla, and us, and see if we can construct out of all the data some sort of image of the last common ancestor. The bonobo adds to that picture a quite different aspect than the chimpanzee has.

A DNA hybrid tree shows that the bonobo is as close to us as is the chimpanzee. The split between the two parent species—one leading to bonobos and chimpanzees and the other leading to humans—is now assumed to have occured five or six million years ago. The split between bonobo and chimpanzee occurred later, so it's not possible for either one of them to be more or less closely related to us. The only debate we can have, and one which currently exists, is which one of the two is more similar to the last common ancestor.

Finally, I want to say something about an experiment that we did in reconciliation behavior involving rhesus monkeys. While I have some affection for the species, nevertheless I can say that it's about the nastiest primate that I know.

Rhesus monkeys have a cohesive group life based on kinship relationships. So I was very interested to see how they reconcile and what they do, mainly grooming. They don't have the specialized gestures for reconciliation that you see in, for example, chimpanzees and many other species. We did an experiment to see how flexible rhesus reconcilation behavior is.

We have a dualistic tendency to say, "We are here and animals are there. We are different from animals." Or, "We are cultural beings and animals are instinctive," as if these things are opposed to each other, rather than intertwined. I would say that since primates develop very slowly, the chimpanzee for maybe 12 years, the macaque maybe five years, that there is time for a lot of learning to take place. That applies to us and equally to all the other primates. Believing that social learning is extremely important, I have always assumed that peace making and reconciliation are learned social skills. I wanted to do an experiment on that.

The experiment was as follows. We took some stumptail macaques which are very closely related to rhesus. However, they're much friendlier and much more tolerant; they reconcile three times more often than the rhesus; they groom each other three times more often; they have lots of squabbles just like rhesus do, but they don't bite as much as rhesus do. They are a more tolerant, less violent species than the rhesus.

Then we co-housed some juveniles of the two species. We had a five-month period in which a number of young rhesus monkeys were housed together day and night with a number of juvenile stumptail macaques. We selected stumptails who were a bit older so that they were going to be dominant, assuming that the rhesus would learn more from dominant and older individuals than the other way around. Initially the two species were segregated and would sleep in different corners of their cage. By the end of the study they were completely mixed. Five months is a long time; it's a bit like putting a human child for two years in my chimpanzee colony which, I can assure you, will change the child considerably!

Then we split them up again. We looked at the eight rhesus monkeys who went through this whole procedure as a group and asked whether they were affected by it. We compared them to a control group exactly the same, but with all rhesus, no stumptails. In terms of age and sex and duration, everything is matched; but there are no stumptails present in this study. We found that the rhesus controls reconciled at the same rate throughout the experiment, when they were co-housed and when they were separate. The stumptails, as expected, continued to reconcile at a very high rate. The rhesus subjects housed with the stumptails started out with the same level of reconciliation as the control rhesus, but began to reconcile more and more over time. When separated from the stumptails, the rhesus in the experimental group continued to reconcile with each other at the same rate as stumptails. We created a new and improved rhesus monkey.

You may want to call reconciliation an instinct; that's fine with me, I don't even know what the word means any more. I think all behavior, and this applies to both humans and animals, is a combination of two influences. One is an environmental one and the other one is a genetic one. What we showed in this experiment is that peace-making tendencies are subject to social influences. It delivers an optimistic message in the sense that if we can make rhesus monkeys reconcile, maybe we can make people reconcile.

Let me end with the model that I support, and into which most of my research on conflict resolution goes, that looks at aggression not as the product of an inner drive, but as one of the options that exists when there's a conflict of interest. Basically, conflicts of interest are inevitable in all mammalian species. There are three basic solutions to conflicts of interest. One is avoidance, which is a typical hierarchical solution, for example, when a subordinate avoids the dominant animal when it approaches. Another one is tolerance, for example, the sharing of food which chimpanzees and bonobos do, rather than fighting over it. The third one is to fight, which is aggression. These are the three options, and it depends on the circumstances, and on the partner, and on the resource at stake which option is selected.

Once aggression has occurred, parties can reconcile. A reconciliation will occur when there's an overlapping interest as well as a conflict of interest between two individuals. That's where the "valuable relationship" hypothesis comes in. In social relationships within groups, animals cycle through conflicts and reconciliations. A typical situation is weaning in primates. Offspring need to be weaned at some point, which creates enormous amounts of conflict and temper tantrums by the weanlings. Once weaned, they come back to the mother, which is a sort of reconciliation between the two. Mother and infant will cycle through these conflicts and reconciliations until some sort of new terms of relationship have been negotiated.

I look at this basically as a process of negotiation of social terms. It's a process that we have in common, I think, with many socially living animals. Conflict and aggression are built into the social relationship. On occasion aggression may get out of hand—that's, of course, a topic of great concern. But reconciliation mechanisms are just as old, I think, in social animals as mechanisms of aggression. People may claim, "We are aggressive by nature"—I say we shouldn't delude ourselves about how aggressive we are. We can breed pit bull terriers to be aggressive; we can breed mice to be aggressive; and while I hope no one will ever do it, we could probably breed people to be aggressive. There is a genetic component, I'm convinced, in human aggressive behavior. But at the same time it is clear that we also have lots of natural mechanisms for cooperation, to keep conflict in check, to channel aggression, and to overcome conflict. These are just as natural to us as the aggressive tendencies. And that's the message I want to leave with you.

Further Reading

de Waal, F. B. M. 1989. *Peacemaking Among Primates.* Cambridge, MA: Harvard University Press.

de Waal, F. B. M. 1997. *Bonobo: The Forgotten Ape,* with photogaphs by Frans Lanting. Berkeley, CA: University of California Press.

Aureli, F., and F. B. M. de Waal. 2000. *Natural Conflict Resolution.* Berkeley, CA: University of California Press.

de Waal, F. B. M. and Johanowicz, D. L. 1993 Modification of reconciliation behavior through social experience: An experiment with two macaque species. *Child Development* 64: 897-908.

The History of War: Fact vs. Fiction

R. Brian Ferguson

Once there was a man named Robert Dart who hunted hominid fossils in Southern Africa. Pondering the broken, split, and gnawed bones of our ancient ancestors, Dart came up with a big idea. What separated ancestral man from our great ape cousins was that somehow we had turned hunter. We killed for a living, and dinner often included other australopithecines. The human lineage was born in blood and cannibalism.

And Dart begat Robert Ardrey. Ardrey was an extremely gifted wordsmith, a screenwriter by trade, who took Dart's hypothesis and piled on fossil evidence, and stirred in ethologists' claims that dominance, territoriality, and aggression are biological drives, and pronounced human beings to be bad-weather animals, killer apes. Ardrey scourged the timorous who doubted that that reality was our true nasty nature. Ardrey's book sold and sold and sold, and then he wrote some more which did the same. Ardrey begat Stanley Kubrick's bone-crunching apes in the film *2001,* and William Golding's killer kids in *Lord of the Flies,* and many other followers in academia, entertainment, the media, and just plain folks.

The problem is, he was wrong about just about everything. The foundational error was Dart's cannibalism hypothesis. As Bill Ury indicated, careful reexamination by Bob Brain proved even to Dart's satisfaction that those australopithecines had indeed been dinner, but of big cats, not of some other hominid. One by one, all of the other famous ancient fossils that Ardrey had talked about and that once supported claims of homicide and cannibalism have fallen to restudies. Some of these poor souls were victims of four-legged predators; in more cases, the supposed signs of violence were just post-mortem breakage.

In retrospect, what seems most noteworthy about this long line of cases is how many distinguished scholars *leapt* to conclude that they were homicides. The reason they did so is clear. For years, centuries, perhaps millennia, before there was any fossil evidence to speak of, learned men were certain that our distant past was a war of all against all. Herbert Spencer and Thomas Hobbes are just two of many. Cain and Abel are two other names that spring to mind. This belief is a deep tradition within Western civilization, a myth charter for contemporary society and militarism. I'm here tonight to tell you that the actual state of evidence about the antiquity of war is something quite different from the fable of Ardrey and others.

Archaeologically, war leaves traces. It leaves characteristic signs on bones: embedded points; penetration trauma; forearm fractures from warding off blows (they're called parry fractures); lozenge-shaped indentations on skulls; scalping marks; missing or extra trophy parts; indicators of gustatory cannibalism; signs that bodies were left unburied, etc. If looking for war in a large collection of skeletal remains, the problem is often the "false positive" signs of violence that are not from war. Even an embedded point can be from a personal fight, an execution, a religious sacrifice, or a hunting accident. When you get several skeletons with these, however, the inference of war seems pretty sound, at least to me. Beyond skeletons, there are other lines of evidence revealing war, including specialized weapons such as maces and daggers, or stockpiles of projectile points. Art on rocks or house walls has often included human figures in combat. Settlement patterns include several good indicators, including nucleation of residences, uninhabited buffer zones, defensible locations, fortifications, and violent destruction.

Now it is certainly possible that for any single site location war might have been present without leaving any of these indicators for us to discover. But with numerous sites and good recovery of physical remains, war, if present, should show up. So what does the evidence show about war in human prehistory? Eliminating those nonhomicides already mentioned leaves perhaps a dozen individual skeletons with convincing or persuasive evidence of interpersonal violence prior to about 10,000 years ago. In most cases we can't say anything about why these wounds were inflicted, but it seems reasonable to conclude that people sometimes tried to kill each other way back then, although apparently not very frequently.

Individual killing, however, is not war. War is collective, a cursed practice with definite, understandable beginnings. For over 30 years, the earliest evidence of war has been from a location near the second cataract of the Nile in the Nubian Desert, Site 117, or Jebel Sahaba. Perhaps 13,000 years old, it contains 59 well-preserved skeletons. Twenty four of these, or 40 percent, appear to have had projectiles embedded in the bodies. This is thousands of years before any other evidence of war anywhere in the world.

These people lived in terrible times, the age of "the wild Nile," when increased water flow gouged out a new deep channel, wiping out the subsistence base of many who had foraged off older wetlands. The people at Site 117 controlled the site with good riverine resources, while the region around them underwent subsistence convulsions. Thus, this first case of war is also the first example of something witnessed in many later contests: Severe climatic changes create extreme subsistence stress, which is accompanied by violent struggle between groups. Not long afterward, the whole region appears to have been abandoned.

The next earliest case is from northern Australia. Extensive rock wall paintings appear to show combat between individuals and small groups from around 8,000 BC onward, and large group confrontations beginning about 4,000 BC. Here too, major climatic change is indicated. After the last Ice Age, rising sea levels from 12,000-4,000 BC gradually inundated what was once a plain stretching from northern Australia to

New Guinea. Presumably that lost world contained some of the favorable subsistence features that characterize Australia's north coast, in sharp contrast to its interior. Incipient, then intensifying war over shrinking hospitable land is understandable. In this region, however, the problem was chronic, not a short adjustment. War settled in and never went away.

A long time later, war developed in North America, well after the ancient Middle East. I am skipping to this because North American archaeological sequences give us better information about hunting and gathering peoples. Some of the earliest signs of war in North America come from central New York State about 2500 BC. The foraging Lamoka people relied heavily on choice fishing sites around the Finger Lakes. Out of the north came the spreading Laurentian people, culturally distinct, but with an identical subsistence orientation. Along the broad contact front of these two peoples there are signs of cultural amalgamation ultimately resulting in fusion, except in one area, where for a short time there are multiple, unambiguous signs of war. These include two young males missing heads, hands, and feet; the arm of one lying charred in a hearth; both with embedded projectile points. But this was short-lived. Even in that area, later evidence points to peaceful mixing. Signs of wars would not appear again in this region until 3,500 years later.

On the Northwest Pacific coast, agriculture never developed among native inhabitants, but war certainly did. Human remains are found from as early as 9,000 BC, but war weapons and trauma on skeletons show up only about 1500 BC, and then in a few places but not others. Their appearance is associated with more settled village life and increased reliance on marine resources, resources which exhibit extreme variation over time and by location, creating have's and have-not's, feasts and famines. From then and there evidence of war spreads along the coast, always archaeologically visible up to historic contact. The large villages of the Northwest coast hunter-gatherers exemplify a kind of preagricultural complexity which in the old world is referred to as Mesolithic. In Europe, indicators of war begin to appear more frequently among Mesolithic people, such as wall paintings which then, but not before, show people in combat. Yet these remain exceptional, and most Mesolithic sites lack any signs of war. That is so among the Natufian and other cultures which preceded development of agriculture in the Middle East. In the Middle East a farming way of life was fully developed by 8,000 BC. Jericho and its first walls appear about 500 years later. Those first walls, once taken as conclusive evidence of warfare, on reexamination appear to be for flood control, unsuited for defense.

After that, picking the first agricultural sites living with war is something of a judgment call. Until recently, the best candidates were two locations in Turkish Anatolia: Catal Huyuck, occupied from the late sixth to mid-fifth millennium BC, which has maces and a defensive construction; and Hacilar from the mid-fifth millennium BC, which was a fortified settlement burned and then reoccupied by a different people. New investigations, however, suggest war even 2000 years earlier in what is now northern Iraq (the mother of all battles?). After the mid-fifth millennium, unmistakable evidence of war shows up in more and more locations.

Archaeological finds in the Yellow River region of China show a similar sequence, but a couple of thousand years behind: agriculture from around 6,500 BC; one regional pattern of (possibly) defensive ditches starting in the fifth millennium, to massive, multiple, unambiguous signs of war 2,600 BC in the Longshan interaction sphere. The Indus Valley and its surroundings show a phased development of war, from a few signs of violent conquest after 3,000 BC, through the relatively peaceful Harappan civilization, the descending into general violence and war after 1600 BC.

Mesoamerica and South America show no signs of violence before the first rumblings of social complexity long after the development of agriculture. The valley systems of the Andes saw the rise of many complex agricultural societies. There, signs of war appear in different valleys at different times and at different stages of complexity. This well-examined region shows very clearly how valley polities with war exported their violence into neighboring peaceful valleys.

Europe offers an interesting case involving the contact of early farmers, called the LBK culture, with settled hunter-gatherers in a front reaching from the Black Sea all the way to Holland. Scholars agree that the LBK people were peaceful among themselves and in their contact with local Mesolithic people. This contact was characterized by exchange and eventual merging. But at the far western edge of LBK expansion, there are signs of village clustering, fortifications, and arrow stockpiling among the new farmers. The archaeologists who discovered this attributed the anomaly to local conditions which made the arrival of a farming way of life unusually disruptive to the previous inhabitants. At any rate, this was around the time, after about 4,300 BC, when signs of war and cultural differentiation begin to appear throughout much of Europe.

The situation was very different in Japan, where agriculture came in from the complex and conflicted world of Korea and China. There the contrast is striking. Evidence of violent death goes from .2 percent of approximately 5,000 skeletons from hunter-gatherer times to 10 percent of all deaths in the subsequent agricultural period.

Agriculture also brings with it the possibility of extremely intense warfare related to climatic fluctuations. North America provides a shocking illustration of this. A continental subsistence crisis occurred in the three centuries following 1150 AD, when drought and cooler temperatures undercut recently expanded and extended agricultural ways of life. Some of the worst evidence of massive killing we have from anywhere is found from this period, including a mass burial of at least 486 butchered corpses in South Dakota, dated to 1325 AD.

Agriculture also underwrites a spectrum of social developments that ultimately give rise to conditions for chronic war, including: growing populations associated with an increasingly sedentary way of life, which eliminates the options for exit and makes territorial gain and loss more of an issue; concentration of material valuables in one form or another such as improved and irrigated cropland; herds of stealable livestock; and trade goods. Increasing social hierarchy, centralization of decision making, and political boundedness, all make it easier and faster to go to war and create situations where political leaders can augment their elevated position through external conflict.

Other archaeological situations could be discussed but would only be redundant. The general points are clear, I think. War leaves archaeologically-recoverable traces, and the origins of war are both visible and understandable. I have often heard it said by those who are convinced of humanity's blood-drenched past, absence of evidence is not evidence of absence. Just because we can't find proof of the war in the past doesn't mean it wasn't there. True enough for any single case, or when information is limited. But when you are talking about a globally-consistent pattern where none of the evidence described here turns up, that goes way beyond stretching credulity. It reminds me of something I once heard from a creationist who explained why so much fossil evidence seems to support the theory of evolution, that God purposely left false clues to humble the scientists of the future.

At any rate, it's not just a matter of absent evidence, but what evidence is present. Again and again, we see reasonably clearly war develop out of a warless background. I have yet to hear of an explanation as to why war should consistently leave behind no evidence and then suddenly be so forthcoming about revealing itself. Humans have always been capable of war, and so instances of war could have happened at any point in our distant past. What happened in upstate New York could have happened at any time. But a limited flare-up is not a regular pattern. It's also true that beyond, say, 20,000 years ago our information is so limited that war could have existed and we probably wouldn't be able to detect it. But that leaves the question as to why that would have happened and then suddenly disappear in the late Paleolithic. If we were talking about anything less ideologically-weighted than war, such as the origin of agriculture or settled village living, no one would take seriously an assertion that such might have existed in distant millennia. The time of origin would be simply uncontroversially fixed at the point of the earliest evidence.

By this point, some of you may be asking yourself, well, if all that's true, then why is it that tribal people observed in recent times, including hunters and gatherers, have so much warfare? Good question, and there's a good answer, a two-part answer. Part one: War got more common as time went on. The conditions favoring development of war developed in more places. Once war became an established pattern rather than a brief episode, it rarely if ever disappeared. And war tends to spread. Thus, there was more war in the world in 2000 BC than there had been in 4000 BC. There was much more yet in 1000 AD. But even by 1500 AD, at the start of the age of European exploration, there was not as much war as there was in subsequent centuries.

That brings us to part two of the answer. European contact with indigenous peoples generally made such local warfare as existed worse: more frequent, more extensive, more deadly. The point is controversial in anthropology today. Opponents have tarred it as Neo-Rousseauian, politically correct. But the position does not rest on philosophy or political ideology, but repeatedly-documented, copiously detailed history. In New England; across the Great Plains; in the American Southeast, Southwest, and Northwest; throughout Amazonia; sub-Saharan Africa, the Horn of Africa; Tahiti, Tonga, and Hawaii; in Borneo, the Solomon Islands, and the Philippines; and in many other situations, historical research unambiguously documents the transformation and often intensification of indigenous warfare.

Why did Western contact lead to more war? Not because native peoples are noble and Westerners nasty. Western contact provided indigenous people with many more reasons and occasions to fight. Population displacements led to territorial struggles. Pro-Westerners fought anti-Westerners, and introduced trade goods and livestock created a whole new system of wants and needs to fight over. Firearms eventually made possible a new ease and level of killing. Westerners directly encouraged natives to make war on other natives, as allies in colonial rivalries, to capture workers, as mercenaries eliminating troublesome groups, or just to divide and rule.

These, in a nutshell, are the circumstances that explain much of recorded tribal warfare. It is this intensified violence that has shaped our images of tribal warfare and of human nature. Hobbes himself supported his view with direct reference to the native peoples of America who, by Hobbes's time, were at the apogee of contact-induced violence.

What difference does all this make? War has a limited history, so what? I think that the knowledge does make a difference in challenging the current wave of biologistic theories about human nature and society. These are widely disseminated views, much more nuanced than those of Ardrey, but in many ways true to his spirit. Biologistic theories explaining human violence come in many forms. They argue that males are innately aggressive compared to women; that our hormones, neurotransmitters, brain structures, or genes make people, and especially men, predisposed to violence, even seeking it out. That aggressive sexual competition in our evolutionary past wired violence into the male psyche, especially that of young men. That as social animals we evolved Darwinian algorithms that prime us to make war to defend territory or group status, or that we have an evolved tendency towards ethnocentrism and xenophobia which make us ready to kill anyone who is not part of our group.

Evolutionary psychology provides a unifying framework for all this work. The evolutionary model both predicts and requires war as a regular, if not constant, part of our environment of evolutionary adaptation. Regular violence pitting one group of genetically-related individuals against another is the selection mechanism by which many of the positive psychological adaptations emerge. It is almost breathtaking to read some of these theorists dismiss the archaeological record regarding war because it undercuts their theories, or else not mention it at all and simply make a sweeping assertion about the ubiquity of war in our species' history. This is especially noteworthy, I think, since so many proponents of biologistic explanations of violence have congratulated themselves on their courage to face the facts about human nature, however unpleasant they may be.

But if the archaeological evidence knocks the blocks out from under these sanguinary scenarios, it merely pushes our question back a step. Again, so what? What difference does that make? Well, a lot. Let me take just one area of concern, contemporary outbreaks of ethnic violence, which seems to be the most pressing issue of war facing the world today. Biologistic writers have leapt to claim that evolutionary theory explains why this carnage is happening, and they have reached a wide audience. I was recently the dissenting voice on a network news story about a book which purports to explain crimes against humanity as in Kosovo, as a product of human instincts to eliminate genetic competitors. In this view, leaders such as Milosevic merely trigger explosively violent urges in the people themselves, residues of millions of years of violent reproductive struggle. Similarly, Francis Fukuyama wrote in the journal *Foreign Affairs* that slaughters in places like Rwanda and the former Yugoslavia should be understood as expressions of the same violent tendencies occasionally observed in wild chimpanzees. Fukuyama added that this perspective was known to have a following in the White House, including Hillary Clinton, of all people.

Explanations such as these come down as pronouncements from a theoretical mountaintop, unhesitant extrapolations of a theory without, it seems, any detailed study of the conflict situations they are purported to explain. Anthropologists and others have studied such violence in great depth and in many permutations, and their findings are no more consistent with evolutionary psychology than is the archaeological record. First, cultural differences and ethnocentrism bear no regular relationship to a tendency towards violent oppositions. There are countless examples of symbiotic coexistence between peoples who are dramatically different. And there are innumerable instances of people who are just the same finding and inflating something—anything—to set them apart once they are heading for war.

Second, collective violence along cultural or other lines of identity does not bubble up in the populace itself. Time and again we have seen these campaigns to be conceived, planned, and coercively executed by centralized political elites seeking to maintain or expand their hold on power and wealth. It is true that their messages of hate have been internalized and horrifically advanced by some followers who do much more and much worse than just follow orders. But to understand that terrible commitment, pan-human instincts will be of no help at all. Instead, one must look at the practical life circumstances and needs of those who respond to calls for violence and combine that understanding with knowledge of local cultural lenses through which people make sense of their circumstances and anticipate possible futures.

Doing that reveals a third way that evolutionary psychology misleads on this point. Ethnic and other identity-linked violence is a process. Examining mobilization phases before the killing begins shows that it is never some pre-existing group of any sort, ethnic, religious, or otherwise, that rallies to the drumbeats. Response is shaped by a host of personal characteristics, different mixes of interests and identity as structured by gender, generation, age, geography, class position, and, if applicable, caste, race, religion, language, tribe, clan, and ethnicity. These individual compounds largely determine who will rush to the center of a movement, stay on the sidelines, or try to fight it. Ethnic or other groups that go into conflict are in reality new constructions, shifting constellations of compound identities and interests which in their politically potent actuality never existed before.

But then comes the next phase, where calculated atrocity and killing is ordered and carried out according to designated social categories, and then whatever label has been fixed on each side overwhelms all other distinctions. The idea that these are fixed groupings with a built-in propensity to violence is exactly the image cultivated and propounded by the political elites who hope to benefit. If we accept that view, they win, because it tells the rest of the world, "Don't get us involved; just let us do what we're doing."

I'm not here to suggest policy options, but I would offer one last observation which is consistent with the work of Bill Ury. In ethnic violence or otherwise, strongly centralized, hierarchical decision making on military policy tends to encourage military action, which serves the interests of the political elite more than those who are called to fight and die. Often leaders favor war because war favors leaders. Horizontal networks among people, though by no means guaranteeing peace, do tend to discourage military action.

The Power of the "Third Side": Community Roles in Conflict Resolution

William L. Ury

We have seen from Frans de Waal a different picture of our primate heritage than the one most often seen. We have heard from Brian Ferguson a different version of the archaeological record than the one most commonly heard. I would like to follow up by asking a further question. If it's true that there is a lot more cooperative and conflict-resolving behavior among primates than we have given them credit for; and if what Brian is saying about the archaeological record is true, how did our ancestors manage conflict peacefully?

Thomas Hobbes, whom Brian mentioned, said there were two alternatives: superior, centralized government or a condition of war. These are the only two possibilities. We know, or presume, that our ancestors, who were nomadic hunters and gatherers for about 99 percent of human evolution, did not have superior, centralized government. We know that they had weapons; we know that they had the capacity to kill each other; we know that in some instances they did kill each other. The question is: Why weren't they killing each other all the time, the way that we sometimes imagine cavemen did? Hobbes posited a "war of every man against every man," by which he meant a condition of permanent enmity.

I'd like to draw on some of the ethnographic knowledge that we have and to interpret it through the lens of conflict resolution. Unfortunately, conflict resolution, unlike war, leaves no material traces for archaeologists to uncover. To discover any kind of alternative mechanism requires looking for clues among simpler societies who have survived into modern times. I might add that every society, indeed every group, differs and changes over time. Since each society we have studied has had at least some contact with complex agricultural societies as Brian was referring to, it would be a mistake to extrapolate directly from their behavior to our prehistoric ancestors. Having said that, however, we can use our knowledge of these simple societies to speculate about the conflict management mechanisms that our ancestors might have had at their disposal.

I want to focus on two groups. One is the Bushmen of the Kalahari, who are one of the best documented hunter-gatherer groups studied by many anthropologists, especially from here in Cambridge, starting with the Marshall family and continuing with Irven Devore, Richard Lee, and their students. The other group is the Semai of Malaysia. Traditionally, and I'll use the anthropological present here, the Bushmen live in small groups roughly averaging about 25 in a group, embedded in larger networks of about 500. They are relatively egalitarian; they have no formal leaders. Richard Lee persistently asked, "Who's the head man? Don't you have head men?" One Bushman finally responded, "Okay, of course we have head men. In fact, we are all head men! Each one of us is head man over himself." Now while the Bushmen are perfectly capable of violence—in fact, each man has hunting arrows coated with a poison that is absolutely deadly and fatal to humans—they do a fairly good job of controlling harmful conflict.

A decade ago I had a chance to visit several groups of Bushmen in Botswana and Namibia. It didn't take me long to observe that harmony is not their natural state. Conflict is their natural state. The Ju/'hoan Bushmen, for example, describe themselves as the "owners of argument." There are constant jealousies, tensions over such issues as the equitable distribution of food, mates, potential mates, and hunting and gathering rights. As one of the elders explained to me in an interview, "It is natural for human beings to have disputes." So the question is: How do they handle their disputes?

I learned that when a dispute arises, they are quick to ask others to intercede. If a person from one group, for example, hunts on some other group's territory without seeking permission first, one elder, Korakoradue, explained, "The injured party will then call three people as witnesses and he will show them the offender's footprints. Then they all go and talk to the offender and admonish him not to do it again." I said, "Suppose the man does it a second time: What happens?" He said, "Well, this time the aggrieved will get four witnesses! Now they speak very loudly to the offender and tell him not to do it again." So I asked, "What if he does it a third time?" He said, "No one would have dared to violate the norms and offend others like this."

Now the secret of the Bushmen's system for managing conflicts is the vigilant, active, and constructive involvement of the surrounding members of the community. As Korakoradue explained to me, all of the friends and relatives are approached in a dispute, and they're asked to have a calming word with the disputants. The entire community gets involved. When a serious problem comes up, everyone sits down—all the men, all the women—and they talk, and they talk, and they talk. Each person has a chance to have his or her say. It may take two or three days. This open and inclusive process continues until the dispute is literally talked out. Why? Because they know what the potential costs of conflict are. They know what hot tempers combined with poisoned arrows can do to the community. So the community members work hard to discover in these meetings what social rules have been broken in order to produce such discord and what needs to be done to restore the social harmony that is critical to their living together.

Their discussion serves as a kind of people's court, except there is no vote by the jury, and there is no verdict by the judge. Decisions are made by consensus, and unlike a typical court proceeding, where one side wins and the other loses, the goal is a stable solution that both the disputants and the community can support. As the group conversation proceeds, a consensus about the appropriate solution gradually crystallizes. After making sure that no opposition nor ill-will remains, the elders typically voice this emergent consensus. Now, if ever tempers rise suddenly and violence does threaten, which happens sometimes, the community is quick to respond. People collect the poisoned arrows and hide them far away in the bush, while others try to separate the antagonists. And then the talking begins.

The Bushmen will not rest until a dispute is fully addressed. "Under no conditions," one of the elders explained to me, "will a person be allowed to go away until the problem is resolved. We will go and fetch someone if he leaves before the dispute is settled. People do not usually stay angry afterwards, so they do not move away." This relates directly to what Frans de Waal was talking about: This is not just distancing, it's reconciliation behavior. I asked "What if a dispute occurs between people from different groups?" He said, "We'll send for the person from the other group. If he doesn't come, our group will go to his group and we'll have a talk there."

Seven years later I had an opportunity to visit the Semai who live deep in the Malaysian rainforest. They have the reputation of being perhaps the most peaceful culture on earth, and their dispute resolution practices have been extensively studied by anthropologists such as Robert Dentan and Clayton and Carol Robarchek. The Semai also make ample use of the community in resolving their disputes. When conflict emerges, people zealously seek to avoid taking sides. That's the key, even when, and indeed especially when, it involves their close relatives or friends. One Semai man explained to me, "It is not proper behavior to take sides." "What is proper," he said, "is to urge one's relatives to resolve their disputes."

Now like the Bushmen, the Semai also have long community talks, called bcaraa'. I was told about one recently convened just to discuss the behavior of a father who had hit his four-year-old son for uprooting plants in the field. It's just not done, people explained. They don't believe in striking children or forcing them to do something. The lesson that's transmitted through these bcaraa' is not only the disapproval of force, it's the approval of alternative ways of dealing with the issue through talking and apology. And they organize them not just for disputes among adults, but also for conflicts among children. When a Semai child strikes another, the adults instead of punishing the child convene a children's bcaraa', like a parliament. All the children sit down in a circle. They discuss what happened. They talk about how to resolve the issue and repair the injured relationship. Everyone thus profits from the dispute by learning the lesson of how to handle frustrations and differences peacefully.

Let me just step back here for a moment from the Bushmen and the Semai and try to explain in conflict resolution terms what I see happening in these societies. When I came back to our society, what struck me was that in our society, we conventionally think of conflict as two-sided. There's the husband versus the wife; there's the union versus the employer; there are Arabs versus Israelis; Hutus versus Tutsis. The introduction of a third party almost always comes as somewhat of an exception, an aberration, or as someone meddling in someone else's business. But as I learned from the Bushmen and the Semai, conflict is never two-sided. Every conflict is actually three-sided. No dispute takes place in a vacuum. There are always others around. There is always some social context in which a dispute takes place. The third party could be the elderly female bonobo that Frans de Waal was talking about. There is a community that constitutes the third side.

The third side consists of both insiders, people who are very close to the parties, such as family friends, and outsiders, such as neighbors, neutrals, bystanders. They play a critical role in dealing with conflict. The third side serves as a kind of container for contention. Within

42

that container, conflict can often be gradually transformed from confrontation into cooperation. One metaphor that comes to mind for the third side is that it's a kind of social immune system that prevents the spread of the virus of violence.

In a nutshell the third side is composed of *people* from the community using a certain kind of *power,* the power of peers, from a certain *perspective,* which is a perspective of common ground; supporting a certain *process,* which is the process of dialogue and nonviolence; and aiming for a certain *product,* which is a triple win—a solution that's good for the community and good for both of the parties.

What's interesting is that unlike a king, or an authoritarian state, unlike Hobbes's Leviathan, the third side is not a transcendent individual or institution who dominates everyone. Rather, it is the emergent will of the community. It's an impulse that arises from the vital relationships—from Frans's "valuable relationships"—that link each member to every other member of the community. The third side, in other words, is a creation of a host of individuals and organizations freely interacting with each other. People can contribute to the third side, but no one commands it. In other words, it's a self-organizing phenomenon with its own natural laws. If each person contributes his or her bit, a powerful collective phenomenon slowly materializes.

The question is: What exactly does the third side do to head off violence? Consider that destructive conflict has a trajectory. Violence starts with latent tensions, develops into overt conflict, develops into power struggles, and then finally crosses some threshold into, say, violence and war. This suggests that the third side does three things.

There are three major opportunities to channel the conflict's vertical momentum toward violence into a horizontal impulse which could lead to constructive change. The first opportunity is to *prevent* destructive conflict from emerging in the first place by addressing the latent tensions that produce conflict. The second is to *resolve* the overt conflicts which do develop. And the third is to *contain* any escalating power struggles that temporarily escape resolution. The trick is to resolve what is not prevented and to contain what is not resolved.

Note that this is not about eliminating or suppressing conflict in any way. We probably need more conflict. It's about transforming conflict from a destructive form to a constructive form. This recalls Frans's model: Violence is a choice. The question that the third side takes on is: How do you make that choice less desirable than the alternative, say, of a negotiated agreement? For each of these three functions, there are a number of very concrete roles that people play.

The first role is that of *provider,* helping people meet their needs. In thinking about prevention you might ask why conflicts escalate. One reason conflicts might escalate is frustrated needs. The Bushmen and the Semai put a lot of attention on meeting the frustrated needs of the people around them. For example, the Bushmen never let anyone go hungry. It's unheard of to let anyone go hungry in their camp or in their larger network. The Semai, for instance, will let other groups come hunt on their lands if they are hungry. They explain that if they did not, "The spirits of the forest will be unhappy and someone might fall sick and die and we would then be responsible." They have a sense of interdependence.

Another role is that of *teacher.* Tensions over conflicting needs can also easily escalate when people lack the proper skills or the attitudes to defuse them. The teacher helps provide those skills. The Semai and the Bushmen, for example, go to great lengths to teach their children to control their tempers and to refrain from violence.

Another role key to violence prevention is that of *bridge builder,* building relationships across potential lines of conflict. Good relationships are key to preventing conflict. Reflecting the valuable-relationship hypothesis of Professor de Waal, the Bushmen, for example, use constant visits and the exchange of gifts to nurture their relationships with other bands as well as in their own. Richard Lee did a study in which he found out that literally two thirds of the time, the Bushmen groups are either visiting or being visited by relatives or friends or strangers. Relationships are constantly being built with neighboring groups, and those relationships serve as a safety net that helps prevent destructive conflict.

Now even with the best prevention, there's still going to be lots of overt conflict, and healthily so. There are at least four elements of overt conflict: 1) the conflicting interests that Frans was mentioning as universal, 2) disputed rights, 3) unequal power, and 4) injured relationships. The *mediator,* for example, helps the parties reconcile their conflicting interests. The *arbiter* helps decide disputed rights. The *equalizer* helps equalize the power between the parties. The *healer* helps repair injured relationships and defuse wounded emotions.

If you look, for example, at the Semai bcaraa', you will find the community of friends, family, and neighbors playing all four roles. They act partly as mediators, seeking an outcome that's acceptable to each side. They're acting partly as arbiters in the sense that they're trying to determine which social rules have been broken. They're acting partly as equalizers, ensuring that neither disputant wins simply by virtue of superior power or status. They're equalizing the situation. And they act very powerfully as healers, trying to restore the broken relationship among the disputants.

Both the Semai and the Bushmen place enormous importance on the role of apology and forgiveness in their dispute resolution. For them it's not enough simply to find a solution to the dispute. The relationship, indeed, the community, needs to be made whole again. The Bushmen have trance dances that accompany their dispute resolution sessions. Every night of a dispute resolution session, they engage in ritual trance dancing in which they call upon the spirits to help bring reconciliation to the group, to restore

45

the community. It's a very important part of the process. It's not just a question of finding a solution. It's a question of healing the community.

Sometimes prevention and resolution don't work: Conflict still escalates. Conflict escalates at this stage partly because no one's paying any attention; partly because there are no limitations being put on the conflict; and partly because there's no one around to step in to provide protection. Again, what you see in these societies is three roles being played to *contain* the conflict.

First, the role of *witness* comes into play: Early warning signals appear most clearly to those who are immediately around the disputants. As one Semai tribesman put it, "We all know everyone intimately. We know everyone's personality. We can tell when they are angry and when trouble's brewing." When the witnesses get involved, then you go back to resolution; you go back to trying to prevent the situation. The witness plays an enormously important role in trying to detect emerging conflict.

If that doesn't work, there's the *referee* or the rule-making role. The Bushmen say, okay, you may have a fistfight; but there's no use of poisoned arrows. They hide those poisoned arrows.

Finally, there's the most intrusive role, which is the *peace keepers,* who actually intervene and physically separate people who are fighting.

In a sense, all these ten roles together are like a series of safety nets. If one doesn't catch the conflict, another will. If two people are fighting, the community will surround them, and the community plays all ten roles. One role's not enough. But you put all ten together and they have a chance. That's the basic methodology as far as I can understand it. There's an old African proverb, that "when spider webs unite, they can halt even a lion." Each one of these roles may be a thin spider web, but if you put them all together, then they can really be effective.

That's what I see happening in these societies. I don't want to romanticize—there's a lot of conflict. There's even violence. It's worth reemphasizing that the Bushmen are not always successful in averting violence. In fact, no society is. Richard Lee reports that the !Kung Bushmen have had a fairly high homicide rate in this century. But even so, as he points out, if you do a fair comparison with modern society, taking into account war casualties and the fact that an aggravated assault which would have led to death without modern medicine is not reported as a homicide, the !Kung homicide rate according to Lee comes out at less than one third of modern society's. He observes, "The balance sheet in this perspective clearly favors the hunter-gatherers, who manage to keep their killing rates low even in the absence of our elaborate system of police, courts, and prisons." Other small-scale societies such as the Semai appear to do even better than the Bushmen.

While these more peaceful groups may be exceptional, as Brian was saying, constituting perhaps only 10 percent of tribal societies surveyed, it's intriguing that it tends to be this 10 percent whose simple way of life most closely resembles that of our ancestors for the great majority of our evolution. While none of these groups can be used as conclusive proof of how our ancestors managed their conflicts, they do demonstrate one thing: that Hobbes was ill-informed, and there does exist a way of dealing with human differences other than authoritarian government or war. And that is a conflict-management system based on the third side.

To put it in the words of a Bushman woman, "When someone says, 'You Bushmen have no government,' we'll say that our old, old people long ago had a government. And it was an ember from the fire where we last lived which we used to light the fire at the new place we were going." Their government is the council around the fire.

One quick word about the logic that supports the third side: The logic inherent in the life of a nomadic hunter-gatherer often puts a premium on cooperation, puts a penalty on fighting, and offers the possibility of exit. For people roving around the landscape in search of game and plants, cooperation makes a lot of sense; that's how you survive. Scattered plants and game are an expandable pie: If you hunt and gather cooperatively and share the yield, there will typically be more for everyone. The basic resource is positive sum. Forming close ties with other groups, moreover, is not just useful and enjoyable; it's essential to survival. If a drought occurs, or if there's a shortage in one area, people can, and often do, go visit relatives and friends who share their territory and food; the visiting group may reciprocate the next year.

Also, fighting has a fairly heavy cost. The benefits are limited because people living off scattered plants and roving animals don't have much to seize. Land is hard to defend, and there's little or no property to steal. There's not much sense in enslaving others, if only because they can escape so easily. And you have to weigh that against the cost, in a fight at close quarters, of someone in the group getting killed. Even a disabling injury spells almost certain death in a nomadic society. In an average group of 25, the loss of one hunter represents one-fifth of the group's hunting capacity. So the group tends to frown on that kind of fighting.

Even if one's group were able to win the fight, it would be vulnerable to retaliation. Among the Bushmen, for example, the poison-tipped arrows often take days to kill a person, long enough for the victim to exact vengeance.

Ages before the Cold War, our ancestors would have come to appreciate the reality of mutual deterrence. As one Bushman put it "I want to hunt kudu, eland, gemsbok [which are all types of antelopes]. But hunting man is what gets you killed." And one of the Semai was asked, "Why don't you hit another person?" His reply was, "What if he hits back?"

The other thing is that fighting usually means killing kin, or the kin of kin. The most important thing that hunter-gatherers have is those personal relationships: The people one would attack might very well be those whose help you might need in hard times.

Lastly, one shouldn't underestimate the importance of the exit option as an alternative. In negotiation lingo we might call this option the BATNA, the Best Alternative To a Negotiated Agreement. It's there, and it's used in those kinds of nomadic societies. Interestingly, the exit is often negotiated. Sometimes, if two people can't live with each other or two groups aren't getting along very well there's a cooling-off period. In one hunter-gatherer group in East Africa, the Hadza, if tensions were rising between groups, one of the groups in contention would—and this is the anthropologist's quote—"suddenly realize that the berries were better elsewhere," and that would be it. Then later they would come back for reconciliation.

I suspect that our ancestors learned to handle their differences cooperatively in much the same tentative way that participants in our prisoners'-dilemma games do. They made occasional mistakes; they experienced the cost of fights. When their conflicts became acute or the temptations too strong, some of them may have succumbed to fighting. Some of the evidence points to that. Maybe some of them fought a battle here and there. But as long as the basic logic of cooperation remained strong, you would imagine that those groups who discovered war would eventually have rediscovered the virtues of co-existence. I think that's what may explain some of the archaeological patterns that Brian mentioned.

What I take away from Professor de Waal's talk is the sheer variation of behavior among different species, as he pointed out, such as between the bonobos and the chimps; among different groups of the same species; and among different circumstances. Our primate relatives are far from being genetic automatons. They appear to be social tacticians just like us, according to his model. They have a repertoire of behaviors for dealing with conflict, and they appear to choose the behavior that's most advantageous to their interests. If chimpanzees can exert such a high degree of control, imagine how much more can be exercised by a creature with an even more developed brain.

Like chimpanzee behavior, human behavior is extraordinarily flexible, as reflected in the extreme variation in societal rates of violence. Some indigenous cultures, like the Waorani of Ecuador, manifest levels of violence as much as 1,000 times higher than, say, the Semai of Malaysia. Consider the modern-day contrast between England and Colombia, more than 50 times more violent.

The level of variation alone suggests that far more than human nature is at play. One doesn't find whole societies, for instance, that eat or make love even 10 times more often than others, let alone 1,000 times. It does suggest that the variation derives in great measure from how people choose to deal with their differences. Violence is not an autonomous phenomenon; it's a choice. It's one choice among many for handling disputes. People are constantly coping with conflicts, their own and those of others, making choices as to which procedures to use. Human beings, in other words, are conflict managers.

My speculative hypothesis about our past is that the reason why archaeologists have found so little evidence of organized violence during the first 99 percent of human history may in fact be the obvious one, which is we've been maligning our ancestors. They weren't cavemen looking to bash every stranger over the head. Rather, most, if not all of the time, they were working hard at co-existing. They were working hard at reconciling. They sought to get along with each other and their neighbors, and by and large they appear to have succeeded. Conflict was probably endemic; we probably had a lot of interpersonal fights; we probably had some impulsive murder; maybe even an occasional feud. But there was probably very little war to exterminate or conquer other groups, the practice that threatens our species today.

That our ancestors were quite capable of violence, that they had the ability all along to make war, and that they undoubtedly had many conflicts, make their feat of coexisting all the more remarkable. They

50

would have had to work very hard and courageously to prevent conflicts from arising, to resolve difficult issues, and to contain violent conflicts. One of the keys of their success, I'm persuaded, was a powerful third side, the community. Their peace was not a peace of the weak; it was a peace of the brave.

Human nature is not inherently peaceful; humans are capable of both peace and war. We know that from our daily lives. Most of us, although you wouldn't think this from looking at the media, live most of our lives in a condition of peace. Violence is not the norm. Peace actually is the norm. If you went out into the streets of Cambridge right now, and you looked around, you'd see a lot of peaceful behavior going on. You'd see a little bit of aggressive behavior, but it would be, as Frans was pointing out, less than five percent or far less than that. While we're not by nature killer apes, we're not naturally peaceful either. Rather, we're capable of both destructive and constructive responses to our differences; we have the capacity to choose. As a Semai elder once remarked to me, "Conflict is created by human beings and thus can be controlled by human beings."

Perhaps it's my bias, coming from the field of negotiation, but the image that comes to my mind for human nature is neither the killer ape, nor the noble savage, but that of ordinary people who are prone to conflict, struggling for the most part to cope with it, to resolve it. In other words, they're trying to co-exist. If anything then, we human beings are homo negotiator.

Let me end by drawing a few implications for today, and just give two examples of the third side at work. I think that we're living in a time of transition. It turns out that how we get along is heavily influenced by the conditions under which we live. One of the things that makes it easier for simple hunter-gatherers to learn how to resolve their conflicts is that their basic resource tends to be an expandable pie. Both sides of a conflict tend to lose if they fight. In this situation, the basic form of organization is an open network, and the basic form of decision making is negotiation which tends to allow people to co-exist.

When people start to settle down and engage in agriculture, the base resource becomes land or power, which is a fixed pie. More land for me means less land for you; more power for me means less power for you. The basic form of organization tends to become vertical, pyramidal. It becomes closed as the exit option disappears. The basic form of decision making tends to be orders, people on the top of the pyramid giving orders to people on the bottom. This produces a lot of violence.

In our emerging global knowledge societies, the basic resource is shifting from land to knowledge, another expandable pie. If I give you my land, I have less land. But if I give you my knowledge, I don't thereby have less knowledge. The logic of conflict seems to be changing. I think that's part of the reason why there is so much interest today in negotiation and in negotiation theories that are cooperative.

The basic form of organization is also shifting away from a closed pyramid to more of an open network. It still has a long way to go, but the internet, for example, is a prime example of an open network. The basic form of decision making today in many organizations, whether in business, in politics, or in the family, is shifting from people giving orders from top to bottom towards negotiated decision making. It's becoming the more common form of decision making. This doesn't mean we go straight to co-existence by any means, but it does offer us the opportunity to learn.

We are now in the infancy of that learning, and a great many of you here in the room are participants in looking for ways to learn to live together at this point. It doesn't mean that we're heading towards peace necessarily. There's no certainty. Conflicts may well get worse, particularly in the short run. In times of transition there's more conflict. However, there may be a real opportunity here. Let me offer two examples of how this opportunity could be followed up on with the use of the third side.

What happened in South Africa reflects the influence of the third-side. When I was in South Africa in the late 1980s, everyone thought it was going to be one of the worst civil strife areas in the world and it was going to go on forever. But that situation turned around because there were insiders and outsiders who formed the third side. Mandela and de Klerk, in a sense, were not just advocates for their sides; they joined together and formed a new center. They were supported by the business communities, the churches, the entire civil society. Everyone got involved. In that process, peace committees at every level of the society were working to prevent and resolve violence in the transitional period.

And they were supported by outsiders from university students who protested to church groups and governments. Economic sanctions were imposed. In the words of Archbishop Desmond Tutu, "You must believe that this spectacular victory over apartheid would have been totally, totally impossible had we not been supported so remarkably by the international community."

The second example of the third side comes from right here in Boston. Teenage violence in this city was at an epidemic high in the early 1990s. It had tripled over ten years. In 1992 there were 20 killings, for example. And then what happened? By 1996, in those four years, the rate of killings fell from 20 to zero. Why? Because the community got involved, the third side. It wasn't just the police taking some guns away. The ministers got involved. The parents and the teachers identified who was at risk. The business community got involved, creating over 10,000 after-school jobs. There were ex-gang members who served as counselors and tried to teach their peers other ways of dispute resolution. Everyone got involved. In the words of the Boston police commissioner, "What was the key? Collaboration." It was the fact that everyone got together. That was the third side at work here at home, in another context.

To conclude then, conditions for co-existence may be gradually ripening with the spread of the knowledge revolution, despite all the obvious dangers it also brings. We're beginning to learn some fundamental lessons about mobilizing the third side and all its roles. We have a long way to go yet. Peace is, in fact, a harder task than war in many respects. But based on what we've heard tonight and on the changes that we've seen in the last 20 years in the growth, for example, of the infant field of negotiation and conflict resolution, in which many of you here are engaged as actual third-siders, I remain persuaded about the human potential to learn to handle our differences, not through violence, but through dialogue and nonviolence.

PART II

The Third Side: Mobilizing Communities to Prevent Urban Violence

William L. Ury

There is perhaps no greater challenge facing humanity in this new century than that of learning how to prevent our conflicts from turning violent. The past century has been the most violent on human record, with over 100 million deaths in war and 175 million in politically related violence. This does not even count much of the violence that takes place in our cities in the form of gang wars and ethnic riots. In Brazil, just to cite a contemporary instance, the death toll from interpersonal and gang violence has reached the level of 50,000 deaths a year—more in one year than the American death toll during the entire Vietnam War—and the great majority of it takes place in a few major cities like Rio and Sao Paulo. The question for us tonight is about how to prevent such violence.

This section reflects the second of two symposia on violent conflict. At the first symposium in 1999, we looked at the question of whether violence is human nature. Is violent conflict endemic and unavoidable as is so often believed? Or is it a choice, highly variable, and preventable? From primatologist Frans de Waal, we learned that violence among primates is not an inner drive but an option, one way of responding to conflict. Violence may have genetic roots but so do peace making and reconciliation, tolerance and negotiation. From anthropologist of war Brian Ferguson, we learned that war has not been the endemic social pattern we have assumed it to be since the origins of humanity. For the first 99 percent of human history, that is until 10,000 years ago, the archaeological record reveals sparse evidence of interpersonal violence,

55

and none of war itself. The absence of evidence is not the same as the evidence of absence. However, it does suggest that coexistence among and between groups may well have been more the norm than violent conflict.

The ethnographic record of such cultures as the Bushmen and the Semai of Malaysia shows that there are conflict transformation mechanisms capable of effectively controlling, containing, and preventing violent conflict. Such mechanisms are based on the active intervention of the community, the so-called third side, which *contains* violence by, for example, having community members hide poison arrows until the possibility of conflict is past; *resolves* conflict through community mediation sessions; and *prevents* conflict by sharing food and other resources, socializing children, and constantly cultivating cross-group relationships.

While in our society we generally think of conflict as two-sided, we can learn from other societies that in any conflict, there is always a potential third side. It may be composed of friends, relatives or family, neighbors, allies, bystanders, and neutrals of all kinds. In short, the surrounding community can play a constructive role in preventing violent conflict.

In the second symposium, in 2000, Christopher Winship, Steven Wilkinson, and I discussed what role, exactly, a community can play in trying to stop violence. They will each present a case study: One is from the developed world in Boston, Massachusetts, which was plagued by gang violence in the 1980s and early '90s. The other is from the developing world, from India, focusing on sectarian violence between Hindus and Muslims. Both cases involve urban violence, but of very different kinds. One involves gang conflict, as well as conflict between the police and the community; the other is ethnically based. However, both are situations in which violence, widely anticipated to continue or increase, has in fact decreased. The question is why.

While these cases focus on urban violence, the scope of our subject extends to violent conflict of other kinds as well: interpersonal, intergroup, and international.

We are only in the infancy of developing knowledge about violence prevention. This meeting represents an opportunity to advance the subject a little, to ask some pressing questions, to draw some practical lessons, and to suggest some areas needing further research.

Reducing Youth Violence in Boston:
Lessons from the 1990s

Christopher Winship

One might argue that racial conflict is endemic to American society. Further, many would point to problems of crime in the judicial system as an area of enormous conflict within many of our country's cities. The statistics are clear that homicide rates are much, much higher in our inner cities. The question of what constitutes fair treatment and justice in these situations has always been hard to determine.

In the past, Boston has been no exception. In the 1980s, the rise in crack use parallelled a major rise in homicide, particularly among youth. The police reacted with a heavy hand, a lot of stop and frisk, what they called "tipping" kids upside down. And we had the Carol Stuart murder, certainly one of the low points in Boston's race relations.

Carol Stuart was a white, pregnant woman. She and her husband were near the Mission Hill housing projects in 1989, when she was shot and murdered, and her husband was also wounded. Her husband described the assailant as a young black man.

In the ensuing weeks, Boston's inner city was turned upside down, and the police arrested a suspect. It came to light, however, that it was actually the husband who had committed the murder, and he committed suicide. It was a very difficult and tough period in Boston's race relations.

Now during this period, the Reverend Eugene Rivers, who had been a student at Harvard in the early 1980s, moved to Four Corners, in Dorchester, with his family—his wife Jackie Rivers, and two young kids aged four and two. Rivers came with the idea that he was going to work with youth, particularly those involved in drugs.

In Dorchester, Gene met Sheldon Brown, a very bright, very entrepreneurial, and very successful drug dealer who became his mentor. He taught Gene what was going on in the streets and why kids were dealing the drugs.

Gene became an advocate for these kids when they got arrested. He would go to court and tell the judge their side of the story. These kids didn't have parents who either would, or could, serve as such advocates.

In this period, Rivers's most famous, early confrontation with the police was on a particular night in 1998, when he heard a knock on his door. He opened it, and Sheldon Brown burst in. Thirty feet behind, chasing him, were two cops. A big shouting match followed, with Rivers in between Brown (the drug dealer) and the cops.

The cops eventually arrested Brown, but Rivers went to the police station with him.

Now let me flash forward to the mid-1990s, and tell you how the situation has changed, and why. In 1990 we had 152 murders in Boston. In 1999 we had 31, a drop of 80 percent—rather remarkable. We now have after-school and alternative-sentencing programs being run by churches. For the last three years the police and the ministers have made a joint effort to deal with an attempt by the Bloods and Cripp—national gangs—to infiltrate our middle schools and involve our kids. Once Boston largely shut the local gangs down, the national gangs saw the city as virgin territory, a great new drug market in which to make money.

Meanwhile, we have cops, ministers, and probation officers going out and doing school visits. This is how they work: A principal rounds up the kids that are most at risk of getting into severe trouble; the police and the ministers play good cop/bad cop, with the minister playing the bad cop. They tell the kids they have to stop gang banging. If they do, they will get help with school, with families, and with jobs. However, the ministers promise that if the kids don't stop, the ministers will do their best to see them put in jail.

A minister says to these kids "I will do this because I love you. You are a danger to your community and to yourself, and the last thing I want to do is preside over your funeral." This is strong talk from a minister.

Throughout the 1990s we saw the ministers, police, and probation officers negotiating about what should happen to kids. I was at a session in late August about a guy who had just been picked up on drug charges. He had been out on probation; the question was whether he should be put back in jail or allowed to stay out.

It was an hour-long session of back and forth about the nature of this kid, the potential for him to go straight, the possibilities that ministers were going to keep him out of trouble. In that case everybody—both sides—concluded the kid was sufficiently out of control that the only place for him was in jail.

In another remarkable story, this past year a man named Sean Taylor was in a house surrounded by police. Sean had been involved in a shoot-out in Chestnut Hill, escaped, and been on the lam for a number of months.

The police discovered him in this house, and he started shooting at them. They called in the ministers and the families, and tried to convince him to give himself up. But he just continued to ramble, and every once in a while, shoot.

The effort failed in that he eventually shot himself. However, it is very impressive, and has now become a legend in Boston's inner city, that over a period of several hours, despite the fact that Sean Taylor was shooting at the police, the police did not shoot one bullet. What changed? It's a long and complicated story; let me give you two pieces of it. I think in this case the roles of *The Boston Globe* and also the Cardinal turned out to be important.

In the 1980s and early 1990s, the *Globe* ran some blistering stories on the police department and what a terrible job they had been doing, including harassing kids. One of the key stories was a series called "Bungling the Basics." It created the political pressure to force the police to find a different way to deal with the problem of youth violence. The Commissioner of Police, Mickey Roache, was fired and a new commissioner, Bill Bradley, who believes in a theory of community policing, was hired.

At the same time, the *Globe* and the Cardinal provided attention to and raised the status of the ministers. Lots of stories, awards, and certainly the support from a Cardinal in a city where the police department is overwhelmingly Catholic was of enormous importance.

To give you a sense of the *Globe*'s role, let me tell you quickly about the story of how Ten Point, which is a coalition of black ministers, was formed.

In 1992 in The Morningstar Baptist Church in Mattapan there was a gang funeral. During the funeral, there was an attempted gang slaying inside the church and 400 people stampeded toward the exits. As you might guess, this traumatized both the inner city community and many ministers. It caused these ministers to realize that the problem of youth violence was their problem, and if they didn't deal with the streets, the streets were coming into the church.

When Ten Point was formed, the *Globe* announced that it was one of the most important things that had happened in Boston in decades. This was an announcement about an organization that was about a week or two old. It had nothing, no record at all. This was the first critical event.

The other critically important event was that in 1991 Gene Rivers's house was shot up. A bullet missed his six-year-old son's head by a few inches. Rivers was forced either to decide to leave, or to cooperate with the police. He needed to find the shooter; he needed to have his family protected. At this point his rhetoric changed. He started saying that some of the kids were so out of control they needed to be in jail.

Suddenly there was a possibility of dialogue between the police and the ministers about who belonged in jail and who could be helped.

At this point, the conflict between the police and the community was transformed. In the first part of the story, the *Globe* and the Cardinal constituted what Bill Ury would call the "third side." In the second, happier, part of the story when cooperation started to take place, the ministers became the third side, addressing the problems that might arise between police and inner city youth.

There is a fundamental conundrum in dealing with inner cities. People want safe streets, but they don't want their kids in jail. However, their kids are the source of danger on the streets.

When some kid gets into trouble, running around and shooting off a gun, how do you choose between these two competing values? How do you decide whether a youth deserves a second chance, or whether he's so out of control that he has to be put in jail? Obviously the police and the judicial system are seen as a distant white establishment that is going to make decisions having very little to do with the community itself. Street workers and social workers always believe the kid deserves a second chance. The kid's aunt, the kid's uncle, and everyone related to the kid certainly think he deserves it. But the woman down the street whose house has been shot up several times knows he needs to go to jail.

One of the ways that ministers can act as a very productive third side is to become an adjudicating institution. They are involved constantly in discussions with police, probation officers, and prosecutors about what should happen. This has added a sense of fairness to the process. Everyone doesn't necessarily agree with every decision, but there is a greater sense of fairness.

Second, the ministers have brought a new language and perspective to dealing with this problem. There have been two languages about conflict in our society. One has been telling kids they have to take responsibility for their lives. It's a language associated with right-wing solutions. There has also been a language of dignity and love, based on the idea that these are God's children. It's a language of caring, usually associated with the political left.

The ministers, as you can see from the school-visit talks described above, can communicate both messages. They're saying the answer doesn't require a choice between these two perspectives. Both are correct: The kids have to be responsible, and we have to understand they're God's children.

What's come out of this is an implicit agreement based on four principles. One is the idea that some kids are so bad that they do need to be in jail. Sometimes this is called the one-in-ten tradeoff. The cops get the really bad apple off the streets and the ministers are able to save the other nine.

I don't think anybody has ever done the statistics to see if "one-in-ten" is truly an accurate number, but it is a principle that seems to be reasonable to everyone. Implicit in this principle is a recognition by both groups that to deal with the problem of crime, at least immediately, you have to treat it as a crime problem.

Second is a commitment to focusing on the small number of kids who are the real problem. The real trouble makers, the kids who are at really high risk, represent about one percent of the youth population in Boston.

This is not a lot of kids—3000 at the outside—and probably only a smaller fraction are really the tough ones. It also shows you why the stop-and-frisk, "tipping" policy is so destructive. Most of the kids you're harassing are not the problem.

Third is the idea that the ministers will have a formal say in what happens.

Fourth is a recognition that when the police do go beyond the bounds, when something untoward happens, the ministers have a full right to criticize.

If I had a lot more time, I would talk about how this process lies at the core of the changes in racial politics in Boston in the last decade. In the 1970s and 1980s, Boston was in the national news all of the time. This was the time of busing to achieve school integration, of the Carol Stuart murder, to mention just two examples of terrible racial relations. In the last ten years, Boston's racial politics have not been in the national news. I think that's good news.

Reducing Hindu-Muslim Violence in Indian Towns: Community Initiatives

Steven Wilkinson

Most of my work has focused on Hindu-Muslim violence in India. In that context, I'm going to talk about four things. First, I'd like to reiterate a general point that Bill Ury makes in his book: Most of the time most people get along. I'm going to offer some hard data from India to show that that's true.

Second, I'm going to tell you about some local level organizations that are at work in Indian towns to try to reduce the level of violence between Hindus and Muslims. I'll talk about why people get involved in them and whether there is any evidence that they work.

Third, I'm going to talk briefly about some of the practical, methodological difficulties that people encounter in trying to assess how effective "third-side" organizations are in reducing violence. The examples I'll be using are from India, but they could also apply to third-side organizations elsewhere in the world.

Finally, I'm going to suggest that when we discuss local conflict resolution efforts, we should always keep in mind the role of the state. If the third side is, as Bill says in his book, the surrounding community that contains conflict, then I think it's important to realize that the state can sometimes inhibit this third side from playing its role and at other times encourage it. The question, then, becomes under what conditions does the state act to do one thing rather than the other? I'm going to talk about the electoral incentives for that, at least as they exist in India.

First then, let me tackle the question of whether the world is as violent as we think it is, and give you some data from research I've done on Hindu-Muslim conflict in India.

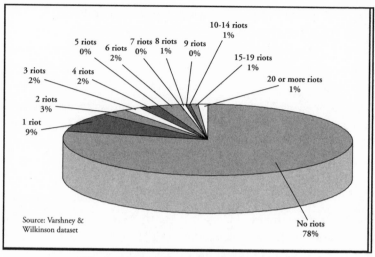

Figure 1. Proportion of Uttar Pradesh Towns
That Have Had a Hindu-Muslim Riot Since 1950 (N = 167)

The pie chart in Figure 1 shows is town-level riot data from the state of Uttar Pradesh. Uttar Pradesh is India's most populous and politically important state (139 million people in the 1991 census) and is situated just beneath Nepal on the map.

I was interested in the question of what percentage of towns in Uttar Pradesh had actually been subject to Hindu-Muslim violence. The general perception in India as a whole is that Hindu-Muslim violence is spreading, moving from town to town and from towns to rural areas.

Together with Ashutosh Varshney who used to teach here, and now teaches at Notre Dame, I collected reports on Hindu-Muslim violence from Indian's major newspaper, *The Times of India,* for every single day, since January, 1950, and cross-checked these with government records and every other kind of source we could find, on where violence had actually taken place. Then I independently collected government and press data on ethnic violence in India from 1900 through 1949.

What the data in Figure 1 show is the the percentage of towns within the state of Uttar Pradesh that have experienced one or more riots, or no riots in the whole 50-year period since 1950.

The data show that 78 percent of the 167 major towns (defined as towns with over 20,000 population) in the state have had no reported Hindu-Muslim riots since 1950, or at least none that were in any of the sources that we looked at.

If you do the arithmetic you will see that almost all of the riots are occurring in 2 to 3 percent of the towns. Most places don't have any instances of violence.

Of course, I recognize that the fact that violence is concentrated in some towns and not others is no consolation if you happen to live in one of the bad ones. But even here, a lot of the data that we've been able to collect gives us great grounds for optimism. The facts show that the level of violence in many towns, based on the total number of deaths and riots in Hindu-Muslim violence, has actually gone down over the last 50 years.

More towns have seen their level of violence go down in the past 50 years than have seen it go up, compared with the earlier part of the century. That's not even controlling for population. If we controlled for the population, the overall decline in riots would be much more.

In towns like Bareilly and Shajahanpur for example, which were among the most violent towns in the state of Uttar Pradesh before 1950, there have been only one or two minor incidents since Independence. If you ask people in Baareilly about ethnic relations in their town, they simply don't recall that things were bad in the past. The many incidents in the early part of the century have simply been erased from people's current perception.

The notion that violence must always beget more violence is not borne out by the facts. Violence can be stopped. Towns can go from bad to good, and so can states. Several Indian states have had similar kinds of transformations.

The puzzle that interests me, of course, is why so many towns seem to have largely avoided Hindu-Muslim conflict, or, in fact, seen their levels of Hindu-Muslim violence go down, even though the peaceful towns seem to be, in many respects, similar to the violent ones. A lot of people have socioeconomic theories based upon particular Hindu-Muslim population mixes, or economic variables to do with Hindu-Muslim economic competition, or the number of refugees from Pakistan in a town. However, none of these theories seem to be associated with higher levels of ethnic conflict; they don't explain why violence actually happens.

One of the explanations that is increasingly common in India focuses on the role of local community organizations as key variables in explaining why some towns do so much better than others. These organizations, what Bill terms "third-side" organizations, are things like local community organizations, charities, or community festivals that bring Indians together across religious and caste lines. It can also bring them together across the geographically segregated areas that so often divide them.

The key to these organizations is a mechanism that was identified decades ago by the social psychologist Muzaffer Sherif. Unlike the peace committees that were formed earlier this century, these organizations don't focus directly on reducing religious tensions as such. If they did this, they would only highlight past grievances, who did what to whom, who was wrong in the past. The things, in other words, that divide people.

Instead, they focus on the provision of some over-arching superordinate goal, something that everyone wants, regardless of their religion or caste. In India for example, neighborhood committees have been formed around such goals as insuring a proper electricity supply, clean water, or better service from local government officials.

In some cases, such as in the gritty textile manufacturing town of Bhiwandi in western India, these local neighborhood committees are only five or ten years old. But by working together, people already seem to have made some concrete improvements in the local necessities of life. They've also organized things such as joint sports events, intracommunity celebrations, and major religious festivals. These things seem to have paid dividends in terms of intracommunity trust and a lack of violence.

Local officials and citizens in Bhiwandi said that because of the trust and social ties built up through the neighborhood committees, Hindus and Muslims are now much less likely to believe rumors about the other community or to misinterpret a random event, for example a Hindu cyclist accidentally knocking over a Muslim pedestrian when he is carrying a copy of the Koran. They are much less likely to interpret events like this in negative terms.

Many locals believe that the local communities in Bhiwandi helped the city, which had, in the past, suffered from some of Western India's most damaging riots, to escape the violence that afflicted the nearby city of Bombay during 1992 and 1993, after the destruction of the Mosque at Ayodhya in Northern India by Hindu militants.

Other examples of this kind of local organizations can be found in towns throughout India. in some cases, like Bhiwandi, or in the North Indian city of Meerut, they are started and encouraged by local officials, anxious to reduce the tensions in cities that have bad reputations for Hindu-Muslim violence. In return for participating in the committees, what does the individual citizen get?

One benefit is that local officials offer people help in dealing with the local bureaucracy, and with things like water supply. The officials are trying to offer incentives that counteract the more familiar incentives we can think of for people to join in ethnic violence. There is an incentive for people to participate in community efforts that aren't violent.

In other instances, community organizations are started more spontaneously by local people, as in the example we have just heard from Boston. These are initiated by individuals who, in many cases, seem to have nothing material in particular to gain from their efforts, but just want to establish ties between members of communities often at odds with each other.

One example is in the town of Bareilly, where I spent time in the mid-1990s with Shabbhu Mian the keeper of a Muslim shrine in the heart of the old city. Shabbhu Mian's philosophy is that people hurt less when they work, live, enjoy life, and interact with each other. One of the ways he tries to help intercommunity relations in Bareilly is by organizing a yearly two-night music and cultural festival at his shrine.

The performers at this festival, which is held from 8:00 pm until the call for morning prayers comes in the morning at 5:30 am, are nationally known musicians. The year that I attended, the festival attracted around 350 people on the first night and around 500 on the second night, with a thoroughly integrated crowd of people attending the proceedings.

Most of the people I spoke to had taken a lot of time out of their schedules to come in to the heart of the Muslim old city. In many cases, these were people who would never have come from the Hindu parts of the city, had it not been for a festival like this.

Groups of Hindus and Muslims seemed to mix easily at the occasion, brought together by their common love of many of the musical traditions of North India. I got a real sense of how the social links, weak though they are, but reinforced through occasions like this, can perhaps be called upon if some tension or threat to the city is going to emerge at a future date.

Local intercommunity organizations are frequently started as a result of the activities of nongovernmental organizations (NGOs). They are often funded by Indian or international government and foundation grants.

One NGO for example, Disha, works in Uttar Pradesh's Saharanpur district, building local women's organizations that are dedicated to improving local health and sanitation. As a result of Disha's work on these issues, the organization has also found that there has been a positive externality, a positive effect on local relations.

In one village, before a particular Disha health project started, the women from the Muslim neighborhood simply didn't speak to the women from the Hindu part of the village. In the initial stages of building relationships in the village, the NGO workers realized the importance of drawing the communities together, but they didn't want to push things too far, too fast.

They offered to hold separate meetings in the two hamlets of the village, but they did make it a point to mention snippets of information about what the people in the other hamlets were doing as a way to encourage some kind of interest in that way.

Gradually women from both the areas started to attend the meetings and became friendly, or at least developed some level of trust with each other. As a result of this ground work, the NGO workers found it easier to achieve the goals of getting people to come together on common issues, things such as ration cards, which are the key to many resources in India.

Once the barrier was broken, it seemed to help a great deal. Joint meetings began to be alternated between the communities' areas. Women mobilized by Disha in the district also seemed to have a direct effect in stopping conflict in the outbreak of 1990 when there was a large-scale mobilization over the issue of the Ayodhya Mosque. This was prior to the destruction of the mosque which occurred on December 6, 1992.

Hindu women who had met Muslims through social work persuaded local Hindus to reassure Muslims, who were very scared, that there was not going to be a pogrom against them. They told those about to flee their homes that they would be in no danger if they stayed.

Because I find these local organizations so fascinating, and because I think there is so much worthwhile in what they do, I thought a lot about the difficulties of showing how we can prove that they actually worked.

I went to India in the 1990s thinking it would be really easy to test the effectiveness of third-side organizations. I can tell you, it's not. I will tell you some of the general difficulties in measuring how much good these organizations do.

First, there is always the argument that the organizations haven't really succeeded in reducing violence, because violence in towns like Bareilly or Bhiwandi would have diminished anyway. Typically when NGOs or governments set up projects like this, they don't create controlled experiments, choosing samples of towns with violence and without violence. That's not the way these things get done. So we typically don't have the kind of information that would allow us to compare, in a social scientific way, exactly how effective they are.

Second, some leaders and members of third-side groups themselves have an interest in overstating the effectiveness of their activities to get public recognition and foundation grants. For example, one thing I noticed when I was reading through NGO grant proposals in India is that some of these groups seemed to be doing very similar things year by year, but framing their goals and achievements very differently, based on their perception of which kinds of issues were hot in the donor community in a particular year.

A project that starts off being devoted to providing water or electricity in one particular place a few years later claims to be addressing gender inequality by providing all of these benefits. A few years later on, these great things are also helping interethnic bridge building. Meanwhile, it's hard to see from reading the report how the actual project has changed. It may be that the project has indeed achieved all these good things, but there is also definitely an interest in framing goals in a way that is going to garner continued support from government agencies and NGOs. This effect makes it difficult to work out how effective these organizations are.

Third, in many cases in India, and probably elsewhere, it's difficult to isolate the effects of the third-side organizations because these groups have often thrived in places where there has also been an improvement in the state's attitude and effectiveness in preventing violence.

In a town like Lucknow, which is the capital of Uttar Pradesh, it's difficult to determine whether the relative absence of violence in the early 1990s was due to the work of civic organizations—and I've had people in Lucknow civic organizations tell me that it was—or whether it was due to the tough law-and-order stance of the district magistrate at the time, Ashok Priyadarshi. He told me that he had been given a mandate by the state to get tough and make preventive arrests.

Lastly, I'd like to talk about the role of the political community, the state. In Bill's book he highlights the role of the community in providing protection to those who lack it. Many of the examples he uses are local communities coming together to prevent violence.

However, to round out the analysis, we also have to consider the third side working through democratic institutions and look at the actions of the state. There are a couple of ways in which the actions of the state are important.

First, the state can, if it wishes, really interfere with the effectiveness of third side activities. You've only got to look at a place like Pakistan and compare its transition to democracy to a place like Bangladesh. In Pakistan, there is no absence of civic organizations, lawyers' groups, doctors' groups, community organizations, who want to come out and speak on the issues. It's not that the basic impulse of the third side isn't there. However, if you go out and protest what the state is doing, its police are going to shoot at you and arrest you. They're not going to protect you from anyone who want to get at you.

This kind of thing hasn't happened in Bangladesh, or at least not to the degree that it has in Pakistan. This is one of the reasons that, when people assess civil society, they say Pakistan is weak and Bangladesh is strong. The state is acting differently towards civil society in one place compared to the other.

The other way in which it's important to influence the state is to encourage it directly to prevent violence. People can put so much political pressure on the state that it will order its representatives to stop violence.

Figure 2 shows state-level data on all the Hindu-Muslim violence reported from 1950 to 1993 in India's major newspaper, *The Times of India*. As you can see, there is a huge variation among different Indian states, once you control for population, in terms of the deaths and riots per million in Hindu-Muslim violence.

You can see that Gujarat, Maharashtra, Bihar, and Uttar Pradesh are doing much worse than states at the other end of the chart. The low level in Punjab might be because there are very few Muslims living there as a result of the 1947 partition of India, but that's not true of Tamil Nadu or of Kerala, which has one of the highest percentages of Muslims of any Indian state.

Some states do a lot better than others in terms of controlling the overall level of deaths and riots. Why? I think it's because of political competition. In southern India, for a long time, competition between Hindu parties has been much greater, much more intense than it has been in northern India, where for a very long time, until very recently, the Congress was the dominant party.

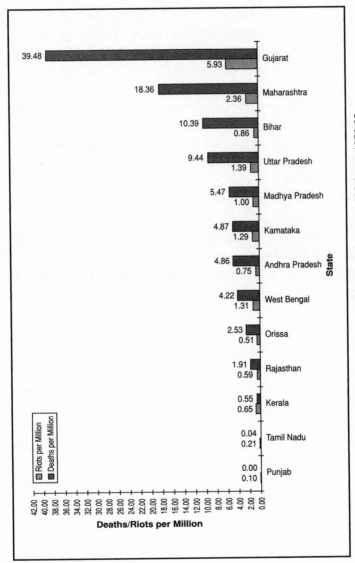

Figure 2. State-Level Riots and Deaths in Communal Violence 1950-93, Controlling for Population (Varshney and Wilkinson)

Having a large number of Hindu political parties divided very often along caste lines—with lower caste parties, middle caste parties, upper caste parties, perhaps a Christian and a Muslim party—competing against each other creates more of a market for Muslim votes. Hindus have to be concerned about what Muslims think, even if their own supporters are not Muslims, because they might need to form a coalition with people who do have Muslim supporters.

I'd like to share one story to make this feel a little more concrete. The case I'd like to talk about is the North Indian city of Mathura, which contains one of the three major religious sites (the others are at Varanasi and Ayodhya) claimed by both Hindus and Muslims in the 1980s and 1990s.

The interesting thing in Mathura is that the third side, the community, had already come together and solved this contentious issue. They had come to an agreement in the late 1960s within the town of Mathura that stipulated exactly which parts of the site would be open to which groups.

As far as the local community was concerned, it was a dead issue. However, there were other people within the state who wanted to make political hay of this particular local issue. They wanted to organize a large Hindu procession that would go first around and then into this sacred site. The reasons were, I think, political—to try to gain support from Hindu nationalists in advance of state elections to be held the next year.

The problem was that if the state was going to protect these people, there was nothing that the local community could do about it. For one thing, local policing in India is the responsibility of the state government, not the town council. The Hindu nationalists were in control of the state in a coalition government at the time, and they weren't going to do anything about it. In fact, it was their supporters who were organizing the circumambulation of this particular religious site in the town of

Mathura. They wouldn't have done anything about it until the upcoming elections were over.

What they were counting on was that the Chief Minister of the State, a lower caste politician called Ms. Mayawati, who represented the one of the coalition parties, would not protest because she wanted to stay in power. But Mayawati was thinking ahead to the next election, and she and her political supporters realized that they needed Muslim votes in the election (the state is 14 percent Muslim) if they were to stand a chance of winning.

So Ms. Mayawati called the party's bluff. She told the government in Uttar Pradesh that if they allowed this thing to go forward, she would bring the government down and pull out of the coalition.

When the party leaders realized she was serious, they backed down, and there was no circumambulation. I'm absolutely positive that there would have been violence had this procession been allowed to go forward because Muslims, although they weren't willing to mobilize offensively in Mathura, were perfectly willing to mobilize defensively to protect their religious site from what they saw as imposition by outsiders. Because of the larger political structures within the state, the ceremony was stopped.

To conclude, that's why I focus on the macro-political side of things. I do think these local organizations are important, but I think they have to be seen within the wider context of political competition at the state level.

Containing, Resolving, and Preventing Violent Conflict: Activating the Third Side in Urban Communities

William L. Ury

We've just heard two very fascinating case studies, each one highlighting the potential for preventing violent conflict. I'd like to ask three questions. First, what exactly is the third side? Second, how does it work? Third, how does the third side get mobilized? What are the conditions which make it effective?

What is the third side?

There is an old Irish saying that goes, "Is this a private fight, or can anyone get in?" In this increasingly interdependent world, whether it's Boston or India, we seem to be learning that there are no private fights because they affect us all. As we've seen in these cases, the third side is the community itself taking responsibility for its own conflicts. It's the community forming what might be called a "winning alliance" against violent conflict. It's the community learning to serve as a container for contention, a container within which conflict can be transformed from destructive ways like violence and war, into constructive ways like dialogue, negotiation, and democracy.

What fascinates me about the third side as a student and practitioner of mediation is that in mediation typically there is one role, one actor. With the third side, in contrast, there are a host of roles being played—with many, many actors at work, as the two case studies illustrate. Moreover, whereas the mediator always tends to be an outsider, archetypically an outside neutral, in the Boston and Indian cases the people preventing conflict are insiders.

People who are close to the conflict, who may even be partial,

Mediation	Third Side
1 role	10+ roles
1 actor	Community
Outsider	Insiders too

Figure 1. Contrast to Mediation

play critical roles in the prevention of violent conflict. No single individual or institution can be said to have prevented violent conflict; the coalition did it. It's a community-based approach with a complex division of labor among many different actors playing many different roles.

In Boston there were the ministers, the police, the probation officers, the courts, and even university research projects such as the Boston Gun Project. There were also businesses, schools, and parents, all forming a complex container designed to reduce the level of violence in the city of Boston. In the case of India, in towns such as Bhiwandi, Hindus and Muslims, teachers and merchants, factory owners and street vendors all worked with police to prevent violence.

In India, there was an alliance between those who might be considered insiders and those who might be considered outsiders. In the

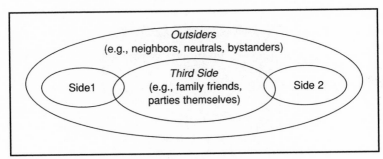

Figure 2. Who Is the Third Side

state of Uttar Pradesh, the state in a sense played the role of outsider; it was more distant from the conflict. The insiders were the local community organizations. It took both working together in an alliance to be an effective third side.

In Chris Winship's analysis of Boston, *The Boston Globe* and the Cardinal were outsiders functioning as thirdsiders between the police and the Ten Point Coalition, who, in turn, worked as thirdsiders between the police and the community in an effort to control gang violence.

None of this was carefully orchestrated. It was an emergent response from the community, a self-organizing phenomenon.

How does the third side work?

Let me offer a rudimentary model of how conflict escalates in order to illustrate the work of the third side:

As Figure 3 illustrates, conflict doesn't come out of nowhere. It arises from latent tension, escalates into overt conflict, develops into power struggle and then, possibly, escalates into destructive violent conflict, for example, warfare.

There are at least three critical opportunities in the course of the escalation to transform the conflict before it reaches a level of

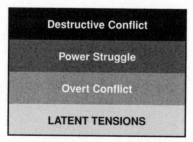

Figure 3. Escalation of Conflict

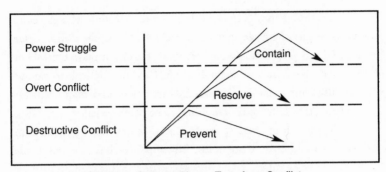

Figure 4. Opportunities to Transform Conflict

destructive violence. (See Figure 4.) At the stage of latent tensions you can prevent by trying to address, for example, the basic needs which produce the latent tension. You can also try to resolve the conflict at the level of overt conflict, or to contain it at the stage of power struggle.

Let me analyze the stories we've just heard from Chris Winship and Steven Wilkinson in terms of this model. Let us start with containment.

Containment
There are at least three critical roles that the third side can play in containing destructive conflict. (See Figure 5.)

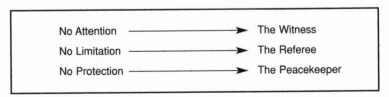

Figure 5. Contain

81

The first is the "Witness," played by those people who pay close attention to signs of escalating tension, and who sound the alarm. As we heard in Chris's presentation, the Ten Point Coalition plays the role of Witness in cooperation with the police. The Coalition draws attention to which youths, for example, are particularly violent and may need, for their own good as Chris was describing, to be taken to jail.

The Coalition also serves as a Witness, as Chris pointed out, not just to what the youth are doing, but to police abuses as well. Gene Rivers built his reputation and his legitimacy in the community by pointing out abusive actions by the police. This function was one of the four principles Chris mentioned on which the understanding between the ministers and the police is based.

In Bhiwandi, for example, peace committees, such as those described by Steven, served as the eyes and ears of the community. When mayhem struck in nearby Bombay, even though Bhiwandi had a reputation for ethnic violence, there were no riots in the town, in part because the peace committees served as Witnesses. They pointed out to the police which individuals were inciting violence or were stockpiling arms. The police then took these dangerous individuals, as Steven mentioned, into protective detention for a few weeks until the crisis died down.

In these cases we also see a second containment role of "Referee." Referees are those who set and enforce the rules that govern a conflict, for instance, concerning what kinds of weapons can or cannot be used. The Boston Gun Project worked very closely with the police to get certain kinds of guns off the street by shutting down suppliers.

The third containment role of the "Peacekeeper" is often played by the police. Chris cited a good example of a situation in which the police were being shot at but did not shoot one bullet in return. As Peacekeepers, they're playing the role of containers, rather than of perpetrators, of destructive conflict.

Resolution

Once you've contained a conflict, there is the need for resolution. This is where the roles that are more familiar to those of us in the field of conflict resolution come into play. (See Figure 6.)

In Chris's analysis, the Ten Point Coalition plays the role of Mediator between the community and the police. Even more interesting, they also play the role of the Arbiter. The ministers show up in court, helping to decide which kids go to jail and which kids don't. They make sure that the formal system of justice, which is perceived as very much outside the community, receives community input.

There are two critical resolution roles which often don't get enough attention. One is the role of the "Equalizer," in which the power must somehow be equalized between asymmetrical parties for a fair negotiation to happen. In Boston, the Ten Point Coalition played the role of Equalizer between the police and the youth. When Gene Rivers acted as an advocate for youth when they were arrested, he was playing the role of an Equalizer. In India, minority parties in a highly competitive political atmosphere can equalize the power between Hindus and Muslims.

A second neglected but important role is that of the "Healer." Healers deal with the traumatic wounds that are created by conflict, helping to restore injured relationships.

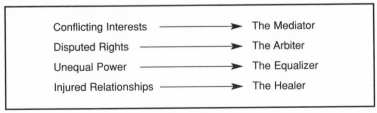

Figure 6. Resolve

Prevention

It is not enough just to contain and resolve. Arguably the most important function of the third side is to prevent. Prevention includes at least three important roles. (See Figure 7.)

One is the role of the "Provider," dealing with the frustrated needs which often create the conflict in the first place. The Ten Point Coalition ministers were playing the role of Provider in trying to address the basic needs of their constituents, the minority youth of Boston.

In India, the peace committees and the NGOs that Steven mentioned work on providing simple things like electricity service, road repair, sanitation, and so on. Dealing with issues of social justice is an exceedingly important role of the third side.

The "Teacher" is a second prevention role that many of us in the conflict resolution community play, helping to teach people how to resolve conflicts in ways more productive than violence.

A third role is that of "Bridge Builder." Examples of Bridge-Building include the joint projects and festivals that Steve highlighted, which build ties cutting across ethnic differences.

The third side thus plays three functions: prevention, resolution, and containment. If there is a motto for the third side, it might be "Contain if necessary; resolve if possible; best of all, prevent."

Interestingly, in both the cases of India and Boston, there were alliances between those playing prevention roles and those playing con-

Figure 7. Prevent

tainment roles. The Ten Point Coalition ministers worked primarily for prevention, but then suddenly formed an alliance with the police who are working mainly on containment. In India, the bridge-building community groups are often the ones that get involved in helping the police contain incipient riots, as in Bhiwandi.

Those of us in the field of conflict resolution may find it a little humbling to think about this because the focus in these cases is more on containment and prevention than on our favorite element of the triad, which is resolution. Obviously all three are important, but resolution may not be the sole, or even the primary, approach. In India, moreover, even the bridge-building community groups are not engaged in direct dialogue about the conflict. Talking about the conflict, Steven argues, may only exacerbate the situation. Instead, the community groups focus on building cross-cutting ties and engaging in joint projects that are unrelated to the conflict.

I am reminded of a third party experience in which the resolution roles were clearly insufficient. My colleagues and I here at Harvard were doing some work on the conflict between Russia and Chechnya in the mid-1990s. We arranged a series of meetings between some of the top leadership of Russia and the top leadership of Chechnya in the Hague and in Kazan. We played the role of Bridge Builder and perhaps a little bit of the role of Mediator.

However, we realized that what was badly needed and missing were the prevention roles, most importantly that of the Provider. We were trying to persuade The World Bank, the International Monetary Fund, or the European Community to get involved because some of the key issues in Chechnya were vast unemployment, huge economic destruction, and enormous social distress. We could see that unless something was done, conditions were ripe for another round of warfare.

What was also needed was the role of the Equalizer. At that point, the world community was not willing to play a role in equalizing the balance of power between Russia and Chechnya. We were trying to do that in our own small way. There was also obviously a need for someone to play the role of the Healer. There were huge wounds left over from years of warfare and centuries of conflict.

The containment roles that were missing included the role of Witness, paying attention to the conflict and perhaps even the role of Peacekeeper.

In other words, there wasn't a strong third side with all of the different roles that needed to be played. The direct result of this missed opportunity to build a strong third side was, of course, a second outbreak of this terrible civil war.

Prevention is key because the third side has its best chance for success early on in a conflict. There is a saying that you can build either a $50 fence at the top of a cliff, or a 50-million-dollar hospital at the bottom. It turns out that we're getting pretty good at building those 50-million-dollar hospitals. Our intervention in Kosovo is a very good example of such a hospital. We're not yet very good, however, at building those $50 fences; we might have intervened with economic aid, an international conference, and observers in Kosovo when it was very predictable what was going to happen five or ten years ago.

Each of the ten thirdsider roles is a little bit like a fence. It's there to stop people from falling over the cliff.

How does the third side get mobilized?

This is the last question. What factors or conditions enable the community or the third side to be successful? I've heard four factors in our two case studies that I want to highlight.

Incentives

The first is the importance of incentives to get involved, whether they're negative incentives or positive incentives. For example, Steven mentioned the way in which democratic power-sharing in India creates incentives for politicians to avoid sectarian strife that might undermine their electoral bases. He also mentioned how local governments create incentives for community groups to work together on joint projects.

Chris mentioned incentives for the police to collaborate with the ministers because of criticism they received in *The Boston Globe* about police methods. The ministers also had incentives to collaborate with the police. When shots were fired at Gene Rivers's house in 1991, he realized that the police were needed to help address the youth violence problem.

Catalysts

A second critical factor for mobilizing the third side is a catalyst. The third side has to start somewhere with someone. People need to start to take responsibility. I was particularly struck in Chris' account by the presence of a catalyst, the Ten Point Coalition. The Coalition, as Chris points out, was a handful of ministers, of whom three were really the most active. Those three were working only part time on this problem because they had many other responsibilities.

Three people working part time were able to catalyze a third side response in Boston when no one else could see how to solve the problem. Nobody was taking responsibility. The police were saying, "What can we do?" The schools were saying, "It's beyond our powers." The parents were throwing up their hands. Then gradually the whole community started to take responsibility. The catalyst was the Ten Point Coalition. This example shows us that it doesn't take that much to catalyze the beginning of the third side.

Critical incidents

The Boston story also demonstrates the importance of critical incidents, which would be an interesting area of study. Chris named a couple of incidents, for example, the 1989 Carol Stuart murder investigation in Boston and the shoot-out and multiple stabbing at Morningstar Baptist Church in May, 1992.

Mindset

Finally, I want to mention one more factor: the importance of mindset. One of the biggest obstacles to the mobilization of the third side may be the fatalistic feeling that nothing can be done because violence is human nature, it is widely believed.

An example of this occurred in the Rwanda genocide, where the third side potential for containment clearly existed even at the last moment. There were 2,000 peace-keeping forces on the ground, commanded by a UN General. Witnesses were reporting on the government plans for committing genocide in Rwanda. This information was being sent back to Washington, New York, and Paris. The UN General said, "Give me an additional 3,000 trained troops and I will nip this violence in the bud." But he was denied the reinforcements he needed, which would have been relatively easy to convey. (The United States, for example, had the ability to transport the troops and wouldn't have had to provide a single soldier.) Worse yet, he was also told to stand down and do nothing. And 800,000 people were killed.

Later on his claims were challenged. Was he right? Could they actually have saved these 800,000 lives as he asserted? At a conference in Washington some time ago, military officers from the United States and other countries examined General Romeo Dallaire's claims. They basically concurred with him that, in fact, those lives could have been saved by what would have been a third-side intervention.

One of the major blocks to intervening was the prevalent story that Hutus and Tutsis have been killing each other over the centuries and are going to be killing each other for centuries more. Based on that belief, people asked "Why should we get involved in this morass if there is nothing we can do?" That's why it's so critical to shift the mindset in order to empower the third side.

Let me sum up then. What does it take to prevent violent conflict? My hunch is that it takes three things. First, it takes a mobilized community, in other words a third side, acting systematically to contain, to resolve, and to prevent violent conflict. Second, this community must be motivated by incentives, catalysts, and critical incidents. Third, the community must believe that violence is not inevitable, but preventable.

In other words, the challenge we face is to constitute a winning alliance against violence. In every situation of potential violence, we need to ask ourselves how to strengthen the third side so that it is equal to the task of the difficult situation at hand. Our focus needs to go beyond the conflict itself to the social capacity that's needed to contain and transform conflict.

We could compare the third side roughly to the immune system. If you've got a strong immune system you can prevent the spread of a virus. Strengthening the third side means not just curing disease, not just resolving destructive conflict, but building health, building the capacity of the community to transform conflict.

Questions, Comments, Answers

Q: What specifically can we do as citizens to help create these kinds of third-side communities? It is very frustrating to think that we have to wait to have the catalyst of a bad experience to push people into becoming third-side players. It seems almost fatalistic.

Chris: One of the important things to do is share lots of stories of third-side success. When I'm involved in conflicts that people tell me can't be resolved, I try to convince them they're wrong by telling two or three good stories about analogous situations in which third-side intervention worked.

Examples of success are very powerful. Bill's work is important in terms of raising the whole idea and creating a language to talk about approaches to preventing violence. It gives people like yourself who are trained to mobilize a community the examples and the language you need to get people involved.

Steven: I would like to suggest that we all think of little, daily things around us in terms of their implications for the third side. When I made my first trip to India in 1990 I stayed with a friend in an area of Delhi that borders a Muslim village. There was an area of wasteland between the Hindu community and the Muslim graveyard. This became an area in which people from the two neighborhoods would play informal games of cricket.

When I went there several years later, a large chunk of the graveyard had been redeveloped into a proper sports complex, with a gate facing only the Hindu side of the neighborhood. Any potential for informal relations between the Hindu and Muslim communities that might have grown out of those cricket games was lost. Boundaries were actually put up.

We ought to think about how the little things in our lives may relate to communication.

Bill: I would agree with all of that. I would just add that I don't think you have to wait for critical incidents. Critical incidents are often the motivators, but they don't need to be. That's why I like the metaphor of preventative medicine—you don't need to wait to learn you have high blood pressure before you begin exercising and getting good nutrition. You think preventatively; we need to do the same thing with conflict.

We need to build the social capacity to contain violence whenever it threatens. One of the reasons why I've tried to elaborate those ten roles is that a lot of us are playing them already. We may not be conscious of it, but we may be playing the role of the Provider in many situations, even personal ones like in a family or a community. We may be playing the role of the Teacher, helping others learn the skills of problem-solving and negotiation. We may play the role of the Bridge Builder informally. We may all have the opportunity to play the role of the Mediator.

I think that you have to find your particular talent, asking yourself how you can strengthen the community you operate in, whether that community is a family, a neighborhood, a city, a nation, or the world. I don't think you need to wait for a critical moment. There are many steps one can take, starting with one's own life.

For example, I happen to be involved in a family dispute because I'm the executor of my mother's estate, and there are differences among my siblings about how to divide up the estate. I thought I could get around this because I can mediate. This was a big mistake because I'm also a party to the conflict. I realized that I needed to engage some of the wider community, the extended family, cousins, aunts, and uncles. They're playing the role not just of the Mediator, but of the Healer, trying to heal some of the emotional wounds that will make possible a fair, equitable, and healing resolution of the dispute.

You have to think of who else in the community might be part of the coalition and build an alliance against destructive conflict.

Q: I want to speak about prevention: You don't need to wait for a critical incident. When I was active at my YWCA in Newburyport, we learned at a national conference that the Klu Klux Klan would tend to go into communities where there was low organization. In fact, they had tried to organize in Essex, New Hampshire, which is only a few miles from us.

The YWCA formed something called the "Citizens Against Prejudice Action Coalition" so that we would have an already existing network if there was any sign that the Klu Klux Klan was trying to organize in Newburyport. Then we used that organization to do other kinds of community building against racial prejudice. For example, we started doing a Martin Luther King Day breakfast.

Because of this ⌊community building⌋ within Newburyport, using the schools, the churches, the entire community, we are ready to deal with these kinds of issues. There have been some racial issues in the schools, and people, including the politicians, are already mobilized to act. We won't have to organize after a critical incident.

Q: Would you talk about the conflict between India and Pakistan and the third side?

Bill: That's one of the more dangerous conflicts on the face of the planet right now. What began as an ethnic conflict has now become a conflict between two separate states that have nuclear weapons. This region is perhaps the most likely place for nuclear war to happen.

It's critical that the world community engage as a third side in seeing what could be done to de-escalate that conflict and to deal with the flash points, for example, Kashmir. That external third side needs to look for internal thirdsiders for support within India and Pakistan.

The curious thing to me about a lot of these conflicts is we give a lot of attention to the few people who are fighting. We say India is fighting Pakistan, or Catholics are fighting Protestants in Northern Ireland. If you actually go there, you find that there are large numbers of players on both sides who are trying to build bridges. They get very little attention and very little support. The moderates in India and Pakistan need to be supported by us in order to form a container that's strong enough to de-escalate that situation before it turns into what could be a devastating nuclear war. It's critical that we engage preventatively.

Another example is what happened in Kosovo. In early 1993 I happened to facilitate a session with the unofficial president of the Albanian Kosovars, Ibrahim Rugova. It was extremely clear to those of us participating in that session that Kosovo was ripe for war. The economic conditions were devastating. There was political instability and widespread human rights abuses. The schools and universities were closed.

Rugova was trying to encourage a Gandhian kind of nonviolent resistance, but how long could the people endure before there would be an extreme reaction and a resort to violence? Rugova was going around hat in hand begging in Washington, in New York at the United Nations, and in Brussels. He couldn't get simple help: economic assistance, assistance in getting the schools running effectively, an international conference to focus attention on Kosovo, peace observers, and so on. A whole third-side system could have been constructed.

Instead, we chose to do nothing at all, saying it was none of our business, only to find out that it became our business. It was extremely costly to deal with, especially after thousands of people were killed.

Indonesia now has all of the signs of becoming a situation that could become as bad, or even worse, than Yugoslavia. It has economic depression, high political instability, lots of ethnic tensions, and a record of ethnic violence. If it descends into civil war, the price will be very high for the people there and also for the world community. We would need many, many peacekeepers to pick up the pieces afterward just as we have now in Bosnia and Kosovo.

We now have an opportunity to prevent war, an opportunity for the third side to get engaged. The external world community needs to support those people within Indonesia who are working to build bridges. The tragedy is that many of the NGOs working in Indonesia to try to build bridges across communities can't get any funds. No one is willing to fund them because the world hasn't woken up to the danger yet. The real challenge for the third side is to get engaged early.

Steven: I'd just like to add one brief point on Kashmir that illustrates the general issue that sometimes people, or especially governments fear that a permanent settlement is likely to be unfavorable to them. That's often the interpretation for what has happened in Kashmir. The UN cease fire basically allowed each side, especially Pakistan, to minimize its losses.

There is an argument within India that had it not been for the UN intervention just after Independence, this issue would have been settled a long time ago. There are certainly difficulties with assuming that third-side intervention is necessarily going to lead to less conflict in the long run.

Q: Two questions. One, I'd like to know what pressure we could bring to bear to prevent what happened in Rwanda from happening in Indonesia and similar situations. How would I, as a student, learn about these situations, so we could stay in touch? Is there a third-side Web page we could use to mobilize third-side interventions into Indonesia now?

Two, are there other third-side failures we could learn from as practitioners trying to get involved in conflict resolution, either interpersonal failures, community failures, or international failures? We've talked a lot about successes but I'd like to hear more about failures, so we can learn from those as well.

Bill: Actually, the Project on Preventing War has just created a Web site called thirdside.org. One of its missions is to alert people such as yourself and to be a place where people who are interested could get in and learn.

The Web offers enormous potential for the third side to self-organize. I could imagine a Web site, for example, just for Indonesia where you could go in and see who's doing what to try to prevent violence in Indonesia: What agencies within Indonesia and outside of Indonesia are engaged in the role of provider? Who's doing teaching? Who's doing healing? Who's doing mediating? Who is performing all of these various functions which are necessary to a strong third side? You could be connected to the Web links of those organizations. People who go on the Web page could see where there were gaps in the system to be filled.

To answer your second question, I do think that we need to focus on successes because the general perception is that there is not that much hope. I also agree that it's important to focus on failures as well. Rwanda, for example, to me is the most glaring recent example of a failure, where 800,000 people died for lack of active third-side intervention. We need to look at other examples, on smaller scales as well, as you mentioned.

Q: I'd like to note an additional example of failure, the sanctuary movement in the United States, which tried to act as a third side for the safety of the people coming up to the United States from Guatemala, from Central America. Sanctuary workers were busted right and left by the INS, government organizations, police, etc.

I would count that as a failure because many of them were arrested and the network was broken up. It's an example of how political and state-level institutions can be used to systematically disrupt the third side.

It's an interesting problem to think about how one can do third-side activity when the state itself is working against it.

Chris: In Africa there is an organization called, I think, Trans-Africa. The idea is to act as a voice for Africa in US government circles on development issues as well as violence issues. I'm sure there are other organizations that exist for other areas.

A lot of this is happening as America becomes more diverse and draws more immigrants from different areas in the world. There is a lot more lobbying and pressure on the US government. The difficulty, of course, is that many of these people have axes to grind—they are parties to the conflict. You end up with the same kind of problems that Bill was talking about in a familial setting.

Q: It strikes me that when you're talking about the little things, either the park that was turned into a sport complex with only one gate, or that in Boston it was three ministers working half-time who were able to create this tipping point, that there's more than the third side at work. The third side emerges when there is some point of leverage that with a little bit of effort can cause a whole series of things to follow. Is this a constant you see in many different countries, that there are one or two points of leverage that can lead to a major sea change? How can we identify and encourage them?

My question arises from thinking about action. I spent the summer at the International Criminal Tribunal for Rwanda, and they are clearly playing some of the third side roles. We have peace keeping, and if that doesn't work, then we just let things happen, and then have tribunals afterwards.

What else can we do institutionally? Because it seems to me that just letting things be at the community level may not be enough.

Chris: I don't think the ministers, when they got involved, had any sense that they were going to be successful. I think they got involved because of deep personal commitments. They are very committed, courageous people, maybe a little crazy, and they felt this was something they had to do. The question of success didn't have much to do with their decision.

The Boston story is fascinating because there were never any meetings. Nobody ever sat down and talked this out. It just emerged.

Gene Rivers has now been working with the police for close to nine years. I had breakfast with him in May, and he was very excited because he actually sat down with the police and discussed how they're going to work together. He has agreed that if he's going to slam them in the press, he's going to give them a head's up first. It took nine years of partnership to reach such a basic agreement.

I'm involved in an effort with one of the ministers, Jeff Brown, and people at the Kennedy School and Harvard Business School, to create what you might call an executive program to bring cops and ministers together for a week from other cities to look at the Boston model and see whether there are ways in which it might be applicable in their cities.

These other cities are in totally different situations than Boston, but it gives them a whole bunch of data that they can sit down and think about and then work through what the applicability of the Boston model is to their city.

Parts of it are just basic. Let me tell you when you go first into these other cities and you start talking about what's happened in Boston, the ministers say, "This is the craziest thing I've ever heard. Do you understand who those people are on the other side of the table?" In Philadelphia they wanted to ask "Have you ever heard of Frank Rizzo?" This case is a success for them to incorporate into their own institution-building processes. They don't have to have the same people we had in order to do things similar to those that have happened in Boston.

Bill: The question of points of leverage is very important. We've just heard that the ministers didn't know they were at a point of leverage. It would be great to see some research on potential points of leverage, what it takes for relatively few people to set up a tipping point that actually gets the community mobilized to prevent violent conflict.

The other thing I would mention about institutionalization is self-organization, of which Boston is a beautiful example. There was no plan, not even a meeting where a plan was devised. One of the interesting questions is whether this is something that needs to happen that way.

If you tried to institutionalize this process, would it lose some of its power or magic? It's the issue of how we could actually empower the third side.

The Web site is an example of giving people information so they know what everyone is doing and where the work is needed, so that everyone can do their little bit as part of a larger network.

What we could really use is facilitation. Maybe it would be useful to have people think strategically about how to facilitate these coalitions. They could identify the parties and try to make these connections so it's not all left to chance, or to critical incidents. Can you proactively facilitate the coalitions that are needed between the critical players that are necessary for the alliance to prevent violent conflict?

Last week I was at a meeting of dispute resolution professionals and I was making the case for the third side. I realized that some of them must be asking themselves: "If everyone becomes a mediator, what happens to my job?" I believe professional mediators will be needed more than ever if only to play the role of "meta-mediators," mediators of the whole, looking at all of the different roles that need to be played to facilitate alliances.

Those of us in the conflict resolution field may not be having a conversation with the people providing social services or humanitarian services, who can be great allies for us, or with the police, or the military. I think we need to think about creative coalition building. One way to institutionalize a third-side response would be to facilitate meetings among these groups and see what happens. There's no way to know exactly whether something is going to pay off or not because we're still in a stage of experimentation.

Ed Hillis, PON Technology Coordinator: We have a couple of questions from people watching the Web cast.

The first question comes from a resident* of West Philadelphia where the question of urban violence is always at the fore of local concerns and politics. The question of preventative programs in the schools is at the heart of the issue, as is the case in many other cities.

Have any such programs met with real success in any other major US cities that could serve as a possible model for Philadelphia?

Chris: I don't know the answer to that. There is an effort to create a Ten Point Coalition and do things parallel to what's happened in Boston and Philadelphia. I think it has had modest success. I think the legacy of Frank Rizzo is a problem for Philadelphia.

I think the schools are an important venue, but the Boston story is predominantly a story about the streets. One of the key things we learn from Boston is that general broad brush programs trying to deal with youth often end up missing the real problem kids.

For example, I was involved in a program called Boston Freedom Summer for a number of summers. An enormous number of kids wanted to come into it. Over three summers, I don't think we got one, and we certainly didn't get half a dozen or a dozen, of the really hard core, tough kids.

They're small in number, and unless you focus on those kids

*Eve Mayer is a junior majoring in US history at the University of Pennsylvania.

99

and have structures that are going to tackle them, you're not going to really deal with the problem. It's not that building a Boy's Club or a Girl's Club in the city may not provide very important and useful services, but it's probably unlikely to deal with the kids that are going to have the real potential for creating a lot of violence.

Steven: One of the things that struck me most about Chris's conversations is how many people had gone to Harvard. These are people who have had elite higher educations, who have social networks and know where the leaders of power are, and can move easily between different communities. This is, in the structure of American history, quite a recent development.

In India the people who are the leaders of the lower- and middle-class parties are very often first-generation college people whose parents were denied many opportunities. But because of opportunity programs that have been introduced in India and in the US, people have access, and they're able to play the kind of constructive role that Chris is talking about. One of the most important things about education is access.

Bill: Let me add one other point to the question of West Philadelphia which is to me one of the more promising things happening in the United States. There are over 10,000 schools in which children as young as six or seven are learning to be mediators. They're learning to negotiate. They go out in the schoolyard and start to mediate among their peers. It goes on all the way up through high school.

Initial studies suggest that in schools which have these programs—and a lot of them are in the inner cities—the rate of violence goes down, suspensions go down, and school morale goes up. There still needs to be a lot of study, but to me it's promising because reaching the young is the beginning of changing the culture. Those of us who engage in negotiation education are often engaged in remedial training. We ought to be receiving this at an early age.

Ed Hillis: The second question comes from Australia:* I know that strict regulation is out of vogue in this world of collaboration and voluntary agreements. But since I live in a country with virtually no urban violence, I'm led to ask if you might have missed a big part of the point. How about gun control?

Chris: I really didn't get into why we thought homicides went down. My papers actually argue that the minister's effect on violence is probably at best modest.

I think where they are important is in working with the police to come up with a constructive way of dealing with youth violence. Police/community relations in Boston are better than they have been in a long, long time.

A lot of the story has to do with Operation Scrap Iron, Operation Cease Fire, and the Boston Gun Project, which were very aggressive attempts to get guns off the streets. The data analysis suggests that they were very successful. I think the Boston story is very consistent with an idea that if we can get guns out of kids' hands, it's going to have a very salutary effect.

Bill: If you contrast the rate of deaths through firearms in the United States and Great Britain, which has a very similar culture, you see that Great Britain has less than one per 100,000 and the United States had eight per 100,000, the last time I checked. Why do we have eight times more homicides per capita than Great Britain? I think a lot of it has to do with tight gun control policies.

*Dr. Peter Cebon is Senior Lecturer for Organisations and Innovation at the Business School, University of Melbourne, Australia.

One very important role of the third side is the Referee. Part of this role is imposing rules for how you're going to carry out conflicts, and this may include getting guns out of people's hands. Parents say to kids, "no fists, no knives—you can fight with pillows." We've got to get the dangerous weapons out of the way.

Q: How can someone going into the legal field take a more proactive role in preventing violence? It seems that people in law are often on the 50-million-dollar hospital side of a conflict, as opposed to the $50-fence side.

Bill: I think lawyers can play enormously important preventative roles. Here at Harvard Law School my colleagues are teaching and disseminating ideas around mediation and the peaceful resolution of conflicts long before it gets to litigation. Those are skills that can be used heavily in third-side roles, such as prevention, bridge building, and others.

The military is another example of a group which is often left out of the third-side process. (We tend to think of them as the problem.) They have a potentially enormous and creative third-side role to play as Peacekeepers. We need to redefine the role of the military, because a lot of the conflicts out there are going to require organization, courage, and discipline—the very virtues that are often cultivated in the military. The military needs to be included in the alliance to prevent warfare. A good example is Rwanda, where the military could have played an extraordinarily important role in saving 800,000 lives.

People in every profession can ask, "Where is the third side contribution that I can make?" I certainly think that there is a very important role for lawyers to play.

The remarkable transformation of South Africa wasn't just a negotiation from the top. It involved the mobilization of the third side in the form of the churches, the unions, the business community, the legal community, women's groups, the universities, and so on.

A very interesting example of the third side in action was something called The National Peace Accord. It started as an initiative from the churches and the business community. They organized peace committees at every level of the society, from the national level down to every municipality in order to provide a container for the political violence that was threatening the transition towards a democratic South Africa. Those peace committees were made up of black and white, rich and poor. They weren't just engaged in dialogue; they were engaged in hard-headed collaboration with the police, working to control rumors, trying to prevent riots or to contain violence so they could have a peaceful transition to democracy. Lawyers played a third-side role in this.

Chris: I'd like to answer the question very differently by looking at classical contract theory. There is this idea that the reason you have a contract is to prevent conflict. Bill has talked a lot about prevention. It seems as though almost all the conversation we've had so far tonight assumes that we have a set of parties that are already engaged with each other and an established set of issues.

However, new relationships are being formed all of the time. From personal experience, I know that you don't always think through all the things you should have put on the table and figured out before you got into a situation. These are often the reasons that you end up in trouble.

Lawyers historically have played a very important role within the contract area. This suggests interesting ideas about whether that kind of role can be expanded and done in more formal ways, helping parties as they enter partnerships to think through potential areas of conflict they may confront down the road. How should they agree to relate together so they don't end up in that conflict?

Q: I'd like to follow up on the West Philadelphia idea about what we can do in schools. Dr. Ury, you mentioned that we're seeing a growing number of schools that have things like mediation programs. You also mentioned a little earlier that perhaps the "resolve" piece is not the most important part of the picture. Would you reflect a little bit more about what those of us who work in elementary schools and middle schools can do to apply this third-side idea in a full way to what happens in schools?

Bill: In terms of what kind of third-side system might have prevented the Columbine tragedy, I think a peer mediation program might have helped. They actually had one, but I think three or four years earlier they had disbanded it. Such a program might have dealt with the bullying behavior, which was the initial trigger for the violent behavior.

Who could have played the different third-side roles, starting with containment? Where were the Witnesses, the people who were ready to stand up and say, "There is a problem here," when kids were making videos about shooting their classmates in school? Where were the Witnesses who could have pointed out that kids were making bombs in garages? Where were the people paying attention to this situation?

It was interesting that when interviewed the police said that someone had reported that there was a death threat on the Web site, but it's not against the law so they decided not to get involved. Just because something is not against the law doesn't mean the police shouldn't get involved preventatively.

What kind of system could have been created in which people could have been Witnesses, Peacekeepers, Bridge Builders? In the prevention roles, what needs to be done in schools, for example, to provide kids with a basic foundation of self respect so that they don't drop through the safety net thinking the whole world is against them? Where is the teaching that's going on around problem solving about tolerance? Where is the bridge building across groups that are being stigmatized by other groups in the school? Where is the healing going on? Kids at that age are very sensitive, and they can take offense easily. They often exaggerate the extent of injuries because for them it's extremely important. Where is the potential for healing in a school system?

I would want to think about what would be an effective system at all levels, not only within the school, but also involving the parents, community members, and so on. How could it become a strong container? I would hope that if such a system were in place you wouldn't have a Columbine.

There are examples in which communities have started to form coalitions with the children. The children feel comfortable telling an adult when another kid is bringing a gun into the school. I think all of those things can be important.

Q: I'm very curious about the question of how to catalyze creation of the third side. What's most curious to me in the story of Boston is the question of how deep an insider must be to catalyze the third side. It sounds like the minister [Gene Rivers] was very deep inside, and on a particular side. At some point he legitimized the other side by saying, "Well, some kids do need to go to jail." Is that the kind of dynamic necessary for a deep insider to catalyze the creation of, or to take advantage of, all of the other components of the third side?

Chris: It seems to me one of the huge problems we've got in our society is all kinds of rationales and norms about why we shouldn't intervene. One of the interesting things about the Ten Point story is that these ministers' religious affiliations justified their involvement, both to themselves—I think it compelled them to be involved—and to others.

It seems to me that in many, many situations, the issue of why the third side doesn't become involved has two parts. One is that people don't think they have the authority or legitimacy to intervene. There isn't a set of cultural norms or tools for them to draw on to say, "These are the reasons I'm allowed to get in here."

Also, there is no set of cultural norms or pressures that says, "You have to get involved. This is your problem." We are an enormously individualistic society in which your problem is your problem, my problem is mine, and as long as you're not stepping on my toes, why should I care? One of the things that we need to work on as a country is creating much stronger norms of involvement.

Two years ago there was a student who was with his friends in Nevada. One of the friends murdered a girl in a bathroom and the student knew it was happening. He took the position that this was not his problem. It turns out he didn't do anything illegal.

That's an extraordinary story about how the social cognitive structure in our society works: This person didn't think it was his responsibility to stop his friend from murdering a child.

Q: There are people trying to create third-side activities around most of the major conflicts. There are all kinds of NGO activities going on. But there needs to be something around which they can all gel. And that's what that incident, the legitimization of the other side's opinions, seems to have been in the Boston case. At that point all the other things that were out there, potentially to be taken advantage of, then could be.

Bill: We're just in the infancy of this idea and we need to think about areas for further research. To me, one area to look at is what might be called "door opening." In a sense the ministers opened the door for the community to get involved. We need to think about who are the natural door openers in these communities.

In a lot of countries it's dangerous to be the first to break the ice. Often it could be a person from a religious institution because they have a little more license to reach out. Certainly that was true in South Africa or Northern Ireland, where there was a little more license to reach out to the other side. Once the door is opened, then people from the business community, or people from unions, or women reach out.

In addition to clergy, the other group that's often allowed to reach out is women. In a lot of these conflicts women are the first people to open the door. They are often the mothers of people who have been killed on both sides. They form those bridges. They essentially open the door so that other groups can get involved. We need to study this phenomenon so we can learn to use it effectively as a tool.

Q: There seems to be an assumption that the third side is moral and fair, that it's there to help, and it's not a nuisance. What happens when there are value conflicts that occur between the third side and the major parties within the dispute, if you can call them major parties. Like when the UN peace-keeping forces go into a conflict area, or when corrupt cops go in, depending upon whose definition of corruption? Or when difficult aunts and uncles sometimes get involved in a personal conflict? Who monitors the morality of the actions of the third side, especially when it's some sort of influential third side?

Bill: I see the third side as composed of those elements in the community that stand for a certain process of nonviolent resolution of conflict. I would argue that we actually need more conflict in this world and not less. And I say that as someone who has spent his life in conflict resolution.

Where you have injustice in the world, where you have wrongs in the world, you're going to need conflict to right those wrongs.

I see the objective as not to eliminate conflict, but to create a container that's strong enough to allow those conflicts to be pursued, and to be transformed from their destructive forms of violence into more constructive forms like negotiation and democratic power sharing, as in India. To me that's the critical question.

Chris: Often when third sides get involved, they have to take the moral high ground, they have to make strong claims about the legitimacy of their position. The implication is that if they do anything untoward it would put them in an enormously vulnerable position.

There are an enormous number of people in Boston, particularly in the elite parts of the black community, that are not fans of the Ten Point Coalition. They would like to see them go away. The Bay State Banner, which has been the major newspaper for the black community in Boston for the last ten years, has reported all kinds of negative stories, particularly about Gene Rivers.

What does that tell you? All those ministers need is a case in which they knew of but didn't go after one corrupt cop, or a cop who has been beating up on youth, and they're history. They will be described and understood as being in bed with the cops, as having sold out, and not playing the kind of intermediary role that they claim for themselves.

In general when you look at these third sides in intervention, there are often situations where they have worked very hard to construct a particular reading of who they are and why they are there and what they are doing. That creates enormous constraints on their behavior because there are other actors in the system who would like to discredit them and are willing to use any kind of behavior outside the bounds of what is appropriate, against them.

Q: In terms of democratic theory, if we view civil society and opposition to the state as a balancing act, we need some kind of conflict occurring between them. The third side allows conflict to be safe. What happens when civil society becomes more involved with the state? Is there a risk to civil liberties?

This may be more of an issue in developed countries, but we could say that it's important for the preservation of human rights in the developing countries. Civil rights and certain principles will not be respected if civil society acts in concert with the state, or with other actors, which commonly serve to protect certain principles.

Chris: I think Ten Point is a wonderful example of what you're getting at. We tried to figure out how we were going to create this program to teach cops and ministers how to work together. I think what we've found is that the hardest issue to convey is how to have a relationship that is partly based on cooperation and partly based on a willingness to be a critic.

I've spent three or four years worrying about when the police were going to do something and the Ten Point ministers wouldn't stand up and say, "That's terrible."

Several years ago we had an interesting incident. There is a Cape Verdean minister, Father Texera, who is an independent Catholic priest. He was out on the streets, not wearing a clerical collar, and there was a fight going on. He began breaking it up. The police arrested him as one of the protagonists, roughed him up.

The behavior of the police was obviously grossly inappropriate. And Rivers, in classic fashion, went after the them. There was two weeks' coverage in the *Globe*. I said, "Thank goodness. I don't have to worry about Gene."

I don't think we know too much about how to construct and maintain those kinds of relationships. They are unusual because it's a partnership conducted at arms's length. Each side is always willing to take you on if you try to coopt them or do something bad.

Bill: The only reason that this partnership works between the police and the Ten Point Coalition is that the Ten Point Coalition has a reputation and legitimacy inside of this community. The only way that it can preserve that legitimacy is by criticizing its partner when its partner strays from the path.

Government institutions, or government actors, can be part of the third side. The third side is not just civil society. If you're talking about the third side as a winning coalition against violence, it will include, in many cases, government actors like the police, UN peacekeepers, judges, courts, and so on. It's a coalition, an alliance between some nongovernmental actors, possibly some governmental actors, possibly some inter-governmental actors.

How do you maintain legitimacy with your own constituency and at the same time form a partnership with organizations with whom you're going to be partly in disagreement, partly in conflict? How do you carry on that conflict within the third side? We might need thirdsiders to try to manage and contain the conflict if that coalition isn't going to break up.

Steve: There is going to be a greater need for democracy within the third side. There has been a lot of research in political science on how organizations like the Sierra Club are affecting democratic participation. A lot of people can't be bothered to go and find out exactly who's good on environmental issues.

They accept the endorsements of two or three groups, for example, the Sierra Club. That's the way that a lot of voters make decisions.

The scholars doing this work are finding that there is increased scrutiny and monitoring of these organizations as people are realizing that their endorsements are incredibly important.

That's ultimately going to put a lot of pressure on third-side organizations that aren't especially democratic. A lot of the ones in India aren't. As there is better recognition of the role they play, there is going to be increasing pressure on them to be democratic and transparent.

PART III

Sanford High Race Riot: Opportunities and Choices for the Third Side

Joshua Weiss, Brian Blancke, and Chang In Shin

The authors, all Graduate Fellows at PON for 2000-2001, collaborated on the following simulation of a third side approach to conflict. It is based on actual events described in the Resources section at the end of the simulation. It is designed to highlight the choices third-siders must make when confronted with an emerging conflict. The simulation is to be used when teaching about the third side as espoused by Dr. William L. Ury in *The Third Side* (New York, 2000). The authors assume that the participants have read or are currently reading *The Third Side*.

Scenario Description
You are Robin Smith, Director of Conflict Resolution in the Schools Initiative, Office of the Attorney General (OAG).

You just got a phone call from a colleague in the mayor's office about a student riot that occurred yesterday at Sanford High School. The mayor of Sanford and the principal of Sanford High have asked you to help restore order. The reason the mayor and principal called you is that your office was created to handle and/or organize people to address conflicts that arise in the school system. The mayor explained that state and local police were called in to quell the riot involving over 50 black and white students. To stop the riot the police used mace and dogs, which called further attention to the situation. The community and parents were angered by the way this was handled. To avoid any more fights and to try

113

to ease tension the principal has cancelled classes until this situation can be sorted out.

After receiving the call from the mayor, and in accordance with OAG protocol on intervention, you called the principal, Dr. Pinelli, to conduct an intake and assessment of information. (Before any intervention is contemplated, you need some basic information about the situation, the school, and the City of Sanford.) Still in shock from the incident, Dr. Pinelli tells you that based on his information a fight broke out yesterday during lunch in the cafeteria between a white and black student when the former shoved the latter. Racial slurs were exchanged and punches were thrown. Friends of both students got involved, and the fight turned into a melee that eventually spilled out into the corridors. The police were called in and they broke it up, arresting 15 students for disorderly conduct and assault and battery—most of those arrested were black. One white student, the captain of the baseball team, was seriously injured and taken to the hospital.

Nothing like this has happened in Sanford for over 25 years, Dr. Pinelli explains. Sanford, after all, is known for its racial harmony. Pinelli conveys that blacks of African and Caribbean descent have lived in Sanford, a largely Italian- and Polish-American suburb of the state's largest metropolis, since the Civil War. In fact, they have settled in South Sanford and have created a nice middle-class neighborhood that is well integrated into the rest of the city. Lately, Sanford (population 50,000) has been undergoing substantial demographic change as a large number of urban families have moved there (to escape a steady trend of increased violence in the city). The high school minority student population of 240 (or 20 percent) reflects this change.

Pinelli admits to you that there have been some problems as the high school has become more diverse, but he did not realize that they were so serious. He vehemently rejects the allegations some black parents and students have made about his administration, particularly that he has been avoiding the growing racial tension between and among students and teachers in the school. He explained that he has an open door policy, and any student, faculty member, or administrator can meet with him to air complaints. In fact, a black student, accompanied by the sole black teacher in the school, did meet with him about racial insults another teacher allegedly made, but the student refused to put the complaint in writing so there was nothing he could do.

As for other complaints made by black students, parents and community leaders, he does acknowledge that blacks are woefully underrepresented in Sanford's school system (e.g., there is only one black teacher out of a faculty of 100). Unfortunately, under Proposition One property taxes have been cut back and the overall budget for staff and faculty has shrunk as a result. He has had to dismiss a number of teachers and staff along seniority lines, many of whom were minorities.

The principal thinks an influx of new students, a breakdown of discipline, and a lack of student teachers to supervise students during certain periods are the roots of the problem. He admits to you very frankly that he really does not know how to proceed. He is afraid that if he reopens the school new fights might break out. There is also the potential problem of whether parents will even let their children return to the school.

As you deliberate on intervention strategies, you ask the principal if there is anyone you could talk to in the school who might have another perspective about what is going on there. He refers you to Mrs. Roberta Benton, the Director of Multicultural Programs at the high school, with whom you speak later in the day.

Mrs. Benton, one of only five black administrators, states confidentially that the principal, while an honest man, is naïve. He does not believe that racism, along with sexism, homophobia and anti-Semitism exists in the school. But over the last year racial tensions have grown. Many black students have come to her to complain about how they have been treated by white students and faculty. Teachers who did not know their names called them "Tyrone" and stood by while white students made racial remarks. In yet other cases, particular faculty members ignored or even demeaned black students who asked to have their history taught as well. She is adamant that the principal was warned about these problems but turned a blind eye to them. The brawl during lunch last Thursday was simply the last straw. Black students, frustrated by how they have been mistreated by whites in this school, simply could not take it anymore.

The overreaction of the police—the excessive use of force—has only made things worse. Now black community leaders, a very powerful and often productive force in the community, are meeting with parents to consider filing a lawsuit alleging police brutality. She also heard from some observers that the police only went after the black kids; 13 of the 15 students arrested were black. Apparently, according to Benton, the schools are not the only institutions that are racist. Finally, Benton did say that parents from both sides of the conflict appear very concerned by these recent problems and they had met with local clergy to discuss the situation.

Benton is especially angry that some school committee members are blaming her for the violence and intolerance in the school. They say that she has not implemented any multicultural programs or diversity curricula since she was hired. She counters that a pilot peer mediation program was set up a year ago but there was only enough money from the city and the state to create and operate one program. Regardless of what others claim, the bottom line for her is that a message of disrespect is sent when black and other minority points of view are ignored. The school system is responsible for what happened, not she, and change is needed at many levels. The city has to learn to deal with its racial problems. Finally, Benton thought the Department of Justice's Community Relations Service might be able to help with this problem. You are unsure whether or not to bring them in because of a negative past experience with them and it might suggest that the state office cannot handle the situation.

What is clear to you from your discussion with Dr. Pinelli and Mrs. Benton is that they both desire to heal the wounds opened by last Thursday's riot. Immediate aid is needed to restore calm and help the school reopen. Your office has been given a budget of $75,000 for expenses and to pay mediators, facilitators, arbiters, and other conflict resolution trainers for their services when necessary. (Some will do this work voluntarily, but their availability is sporadic.) However, due to an unprecedented increase in problems this year, your budget has dwindled to $5,000. The mayor was uncertain if any additional funds would be available for your potential efforts, so you must not rely on any more monetary support.

You have the weekend to develop a strategy. You must decide what to do and from whom to seek help. Here are some questions that will help you to do so:

1. *Initial Reactions*
   A. Where might you begin and what is your logic?
   B. Would you try to get the third side to prevent, resolve, and/or contain this conflict? Why?
   C. At what level(s) of the problem, for example, the city, Sanford High School, students involved in the riot, would you seek to mobilize thirdsiders and why?
   D. What questions would you need to ask people involved about the past, present, and future in order to make this determination?

117

2. *Identifying the Players*
   A. Broadly speaking, who are the people influencing this situation?
   B. Who is the third side and what roles are already being played?
   C. Who is not involved and who should be? How would you try to mobilize them?
   D. Are there any pre-existing relationships across conflict lines that could be helpful as you seek to mobilize the third side?
   E. What questions would you ask people involved to find these things out?

3. *Structuring a Third Side Response*
   A. How would the roles you mentioned work in a coordinated fashion?
   B. Which roles would be deployed first?
   C. What questions would you ask to help determine the coordination and sequencing?
   D. What relationships (e.g., with the media or with the administration) would need to be built in order to implement the third-side intervention?
   E. What are the impediments and constraints to mobilizing these roles?

Preliminary Teaching Note

This case is designed to get the participant to think through the choices associated with mobilizing the third side. The person involved is given the task of trying to mobilize the third side to address the conflict in question. The case is based on an actual situation in the city of Medford, Massachusetts, in 1992. This exercise is focused on analyzing the situation, thinking about the levels at which the conflict is occurring, determining whether to prevent, resolve, and/or contain the conflict, and in what order to think about which third-side roles are applicable and how those roles can be pushed, nudged, and cajoled into working in a systematic fashion. The simulation is also intended to get participants to think about which questions to ask at each stage and why.

As the instructor you may want to use the following questions to help debrief the simulation:

1. How might you analyze this conflict? What do you determine to be the sources of the problem? What questions might you ask about the past, present, and future to help you make this determination?

2. What level (e.g., city, school system, teachers and students, students only, only those that rioted) do your third-side intervention plans focus on and why?

3. Which perspective—prevention, resolution, and/or containment—make the most sense in trying to mobilize the third side to act?

4. What roles from Ury's list need to be played to deal with this conflict? Which are already in place and which are not but might be harnessed?

5. How can you try to mobilize different people to play the different roles of the third side? What arguments/questions can you use to get them to get involved and to think through the issues?

6. How do you deal with the question of coordinating these roles in a coherent and systematic manner? What questions come to mind when thinking through this issue?

7. What do you perceive to be some of the obstacles (e.g. authority, permission, commitment by school to implement what is

agreed to, resources, media, coordination, turf issues) to addressing this conflict from a third side perspective?

Time Needed
Preferably from one class to the next. In-class time needed for the exercise is 1.5 hours with 1 hour to debrief.

Materials
Each participant needs one copy of the scenario description. You may also want to make copies of some of the newspaper articles listed on the next page for participant review after the debrief.

Resources

Reports

Harshbarger, Scott. February 1993. *Report on Medford High School,* Boston: Office of the Attorney General.

Articles

From *The Boston Globe*

"Racial fights erupt at Medford High School," December 11, 1992, p. 1

"Mediators seek Medford High truce," December 12, 1992, p. 1

"Raw wounds in Medford," (editorial) December 12, 1992, p. 10

"Justice team at Medford High," December 14, 1992, p. 17

"In Medford, parents voice fear and anger," December 15, 1992, p.1

"Signals seen to Medford clash," December 17, 1992, p. 1

"Schools and bias: no quick fixes," December 19, 1992, p. 1

"After clash, Medford faces deep divisions," December 20, 1992, p. 41

"Medford faculty, officials need training too, mediator says," December 31, 1992, p. 25

"Students solving disputes peacefully," January 10, 1993, p. 3

"AG faults Medford schools on hiring," February 13, 1993, p. 21

Cox, Debbie. 1993. "Reflections of a UCM Mediator." *The Mediator's Agenda* (Spring pp. 5-6) Boston: Massachusetts Association of Mediation Programs and Practitioners.

Stewart, Art. 1993. "The Mediation Community Responds to Medford High," *The Mediator's Agenda* (Spring pp. 1, 7-8) Boston: Massachusetts Association of Mediation Programs and Practitioners.

Additional Resources

Conflict Intervention Team (CIT) and SCORE (Student Conflict Resolution Experts) are both programs of the Massachusetts Department of the Attorney General, 1 Ashburton Place, Boston, MA 02108. For more information, see www.ago.state.ma.us/child-default.asp.

Convergent Media Systems. 1994. *The Possible Dream?—The Quest for Racial & Ethnic Harmony in American Schools.* (video). So. Charleston, WVA: Cambridge Educational.

The Community Relations Service (CRS) provides mediators to "help local communities settle destructive conflicts and disturbances relating to race, color, or national origin." One of the services CRS provides for schools is "Student Problem Identification and Resolution (SPIR)." For more information, see www.usdoj.gov/crs.